Routledge Revivals

Burma Through the Centuries

Burma Through the Centuries

Being a short account of the leading races of Burma, of their origin, and of their struggles for supremacy throughout past centuries; also of the three Burmese Wars and of the annexation of the country by the British Government

John Stuart

Routledge Revivals
Routledge
Taylor & Francis Group

First published in 1910 by Kegan Paul, Trench, Trübner & Co., Ltd.

This edition first published in 2018 by Routledge
2 Park Square, Milton Park, Abingdon, Oxon, OX14 4RN
and by Routledge
711 Third Avenue, New York, NY 10017

Routledge is an imprint of the Taylor & Francis Group, an informa business

Publisher's Note
The publisher has gone to great lengths to ensure the quality of this reprint but points out that some imperfections in the original copies may be apparent.

Disclaimer
The publisher has made every effort to trace copyright holders and welcomes correspondence from those they have been unable to contact.

A Library of Congress record exists under ISBN: 10015127

ISBN 13: 978-1-138-61496-3 (hbk)
ISBN 13: 978-1-138-61502-1 (pbk)
ISBN 13: 978-0-429-46350-1 (ebk)

THE QUEEN'S GOLDEN MONASTERY, MANDALAY

BUILT BY QUEEN SUPAYALAT IN 1885

Reproduced from illustration in "Some Conservation Works in Burma" by Mr Taw Sein Ko, Superintendent of the Archæological Survey

BURMA
Through the Centuries

Being a short account of the leading races of Burma, of their origin, and of their struggles for supremacy throughout past centuries; also of the three Burmese Wars and of the annexation of the country by the British Government.

BY

JOHN STUART

(Managing Proprietor, *Rangoon Gazette*)

WITH FIFTEEN ILLUSTRATIONS

SECOND EDITION
REVISED AND ENLARGED

LONDON:
KEGAN PAUL, TRENCH, TRÜBNER & CO. LIMITED,
DRYDEN HOUSE, 43 GERRARD STREET, W.

1910

PREFACE

IT is astonishing how little either the Burmese themselves, or Europeans who have been long resident in the country, know of the history of Burma. Although I have lived in Burma for nearly forty years, it was only when I had occasion, last year, to write a brief sketch of that history that I realised how little I really knew about it. At the same time I discovered the cause of the prevailing ignorance. I was unable to find any book which gave a clear and intelligible account of what is really known. The late Sir Arthur Phayre's book was the only one I could discover in which the attempt is made to give a complete account of Burma through the ages. But, valuable as that book is, it is scarcely the book which the business man of scant leisure resident in the country, or the visitor, is likely to read. For one thing, to the European reader, at least, the profusion of native names introduced is very confusing. It is difficult to remember names so unfamiliar, and one is constantly turning back to see who this or the other person is. The difficulty is increased by the change of spelling which has since been introduced in the matter of Burmese words and names. Then there is a wealth of detail in matters of comparatively little importance, taken often from Burmese sources, on which but little dependence can be placed, and long accounts of ruthless wars, of wholesale murders, and of horrible cruelties, which become very tiresome. It is scarcely to be wondered at that the average resident even gives up the attempt to follow all this, and contents himself with a vague idea that Burmese history may be summed up as a wearisome record of barbarity and cruelty. It is that, no doubt, but there is more in it than that. The Kings were not all bloodthirsty and utterly selfish tyrants, though too many of them were. Moreover, the essentially interesting part of the history lies, not in the doings of the Kings, but in the struggle for supremacy of the various races inhabiting the country, more especially the Burmese, the Shans, and the Talaings. This triangular contest was carried on for more than a thousand years, certainly—for considerably more, in all probability; and this makes Burmese history all the more difficult to follow. It makes the history of Burma very much like what a combined history of France, England and Scotland, up to the accession of James I. to the throne of England, would be. Even that does not quite represent the complexity of Burmese history, for the Burmese race had separated into two sections, the one inhabiting Upper Burma and the other Arakan. Moreover, there were the Karens, the Was, and other hill tribes who retained more or less independence throughout in their mountain fastnesses.

In the following pages I have endeavoured to give a brief account of what is really known of this long struggle, as clearly as I could. I make no pretention to scholarship, but have aimed at putting what is known in such form as to render it accessible to any one, be he resident or visitor, who wishes to know, in general outline at least, what the history of the country has been. The books from which I have drawn my information are as follows:—

"History of Burma," by Sir Arthur P. Phayre, G.C.M.G., K.C.S.I., and C.B.

"Our Burmese Wars," by Colonel W. F. B. Laurie.

"The Loyal Karens of Burma," by Donald Mackenzie Smeaton, M.A., Bengal Civil Service.

"The Gazetteer of Upper Burma and the Shan States," by Sir J. George Scott, K.C.I.E., Superintendent and Political Officer, Southern Shan States.

"A Description of the Burmese Empire," by Rev. Father Sangermano.

"Burma, with Special Reference to her Relations with China," by E. H. Parker, H.M. Consul, Kiungchow, and at one time Officiating Adviser on Chinese Affairs in Burma.

"The Alaungpra Dynasty," by James Gray.

"Reminiscences of the Court of Mandalay. Extracts from the Diary of General Horace A. Browne, 1859-1879."

I am also indebted to Mr Taw Sein Ko, Superintendent of the Archæological Survey of Burma, for some information as to what is known of Burma in prehistoric times; and to Mr Charles Duroiselle, Lecturer in Pâli at the Rangoon College, for the loan of some pamphlets on the same subject.

J. STUART

Rangoon

12th February, 1909.

PREFACE TO THE SECOND EDITION.

It is gratifying to find that this little book has met with so favourable a reception that a second edition is called for. In publishing this, I take the opportunity to reply to the criticisms I have seen, and to repair the omission, in the first edition, of any reference to Marco Polo's account of the Burma of his day. All this I have done in an appendix, the first part of which, that referring to Mr Duroiselle's criticisms, should be read in connection with the first two chapters, and with the first three paragraphs in the third chapter in the book. The account given in the Appendix of Marco Polo's references to Burma is practically a sequel to Chapter III. The question raised, as to Alompra's names and those of three of his successors, should be considered in connection with the chapters dealing with the Alompra dynasty. The remainder of the appendix deals only with the reference to General de Facieu on page 153, and with Colonel Browne's reference to French and Italian adventurers, reproduced on page 168.

J. STUART

DOLLAR, N.B.

25th July, 1910

Contents

List of Illustrations

CHAPTER I.

BEFORE A.D. 639

THERE is every reason to believe that the numerous races inhabiting the country now known as Burma are aliens, who poured down from Western China, from Tibet, and perhaps from North-Eastern India, in prehistoric times. This influx probably began long before the commencement of the Christian era, and was continued through centuries, each successive wave struggling for such territory as it could obtain. Of earlier indigenous inhabitants there is no trace, but the probability is that the country had previously been inhabited by the Negrito race. This race is still to be found in the Andaman Islands, near Burma, and extends its habitat from there to the Philippines. It was probably very much more numerous at one time than it is now, but was quite unable to hold its own against more advanced races, so has survived only in places where it was protected by isolation. Even tradition has not preserved any record of conflict with the Negrito race, but to the new-comers these poor people could have offered no effective resistance of any kind. They would hide in the forests until they died out or escaped to the Andamans, and to the immigrants they would be less of a danger than the wild beasts. Any fighting there may have been with them would soon be lost sight of in the more serious wars which the immigrants were continually waging with each other.

The first race of immigrants belonged to the Mon-Khmer stock, and the reason for believing that they came from North-Eastern India is that they are allied to the Khasias in Assam and to the Bhils and Gonds. When they were driven out of India, and whether their expulsion was due to the Aryan conquest of India, it is impossible to determine, but, as they have left some of their congeners behind, the probability is that they came from India. It is probable too that they came first, as their chief representatives are the Cambodians in Indo-China, and the Talaings, or Peguans, in Burma. They were, no doubt, pushed down by the later waves of migration, and the Talaing branch settled in what are now known as the Pegu and Tenasserim Divisions of Burma. The bulk of the inhabitants there are of Talaing race, though the majority of them have become thoroughly Burmanised, and scarcely know that they are not Burmans. They speak Burmese habitually, the Talaing language being nearly, though not quite, extinct. The branch which settled in Cambodia must have made their way through Siam long before the existing kingdom of that name came into existence. Even until the close of the eighteenth century, numbers of Talaings were driven in that direction by the persecution of the Burmese. In the year 1826, an Englishman, Mr Leal, travelled overland from Martaban to Bangkok, and in his journey he found that certain tracts were inhabited by Talaings, or "Peguers" as he calls them. He mentions one town of "five thousand inhabitants, chiefly Peguers," and at another stage of his journey he passed through a tract which, he says, was inhabited by sixteen thousand Peguers. The Cambodians scarcely come into a history of Burma, but it is noteworthy that both they and the Talaings in Burma, in time formed fairly powerful and

NEGRITO RACE

GROUP OF ANDAMANESE

Photograph by Mr P. Klier, Rangoon

comparatively civilised States. When we get to anything like authentic history, the Talaing kingdom in Pegu and Tenasserim was the most advanced State in Burma. Very different was the fate of another branch of the same race, which got stranded among the hills in the Northern Shan States, and is now represented by the Palaungs and the Was. The latter, more especially, are wild savages, who look on clothes as a superfluity, and are held in dread by their neighbours on account of their head-hunting proclivities. Their neighbours assert that they are cannibals, but this is a libel, as their desire for heads is due solely to their belief that their crops will fail unless some fresh human skulls are imported to the village every year. Under this impression they organise head-hunting expeditions every spring, and it is small consolation to the unfortunate traveller who falls into their hands that it is only his skull that is wanted. Tradition asserts that the Was once occupied a much larger tract of country than they do now, and were not then more uncivilised than their neighbours. If so, we may be sure that they were not driven back without fierce fighting, and there can be no doubt that in pre-historic times the various immigrant races carried on as ruthless wars with each other as we find them doing throughout historical times, until this was put a stop to by the British Government.

The contrast in civilisation between the Talaings and the Was, though both of the same stock and, presumably, of much the same standard of civilisation at the time of their first immigration, is typical of what has happened in a greater or lesser degree to all the immigrants. Those who got down to fertile plains, within reach of the sea, or even of navigable rivers, were able to form fairly powerful kingdoms. They came into contact, too, with outside nations, from whom they learned much. The Talaings, for instance, owe their civilisation very largely to the Buddhist missionaries from India, and to Indian traders. Colonel Phayre connects the word Talaing with Telingâna, and says the name was doubtless applied originally only to settlers from India, though, afterwards, it was used for all those of the Mon-Khmer race, or, at least, to those in Pegu and Tenasserim. This derivation implies great antiquity for the name, but Gray asserts that the word Talaing means "the down-trodden," and was only applied to the Peguans after their crushing defeat at the hands of Alaungpra, in the eighteenth century Be this as it may, the Talaings very early formed a comparatively civilised community, while their relatives, the Was, isolated in a hill tract, sunk to their present level of degradation. Some of them, known to their neighbours as the "Tame Was," have given up head-hunting and will even come to market decently clad. The Wild Wa, however, has no dealings with his neighbours beyond the head-hunting aforesaid. In hot weather he and his wife are naked and unashamed; they are filthily dirty, and altogether just as unpleasant a specimen of the savage as can well be found. All the same, they build more substantial houses than many of their more highly civilised neighbours, and their villages are ingeniously defended, the only approach being through a long tunnel, winding so that nothing can be fired up it. Against all the arms which any of their neighbours possess it is practically impregnable. For many centuries they must thus have stood at bay against all their neighbours, and while steadily retrograding as far as the decencies of life are concerned, they have continued to keep up these defences, which, no doubt, originally saved them from extermination. They have also an ingenious system of bamboo aqueducts, by which water is brought, often from a considerable distance, into their villages. They are very good agriculturists, though all their fields involve a climb up or down the steep mountain side. They grow buck-wheat, beans and maize, and they keep pigs, fowls, and dogs, all for food. They are greatly addicted to drink, for which they have to grow rice, which is often planted as much as three thousand feet below their village. But their chief crop is the poppy, and the hill-tops in February and March are white with the blossoms. One can journey for days through nothing but opium fields, and this is a crop which needs constant and careful attention.

The next wave of migration came from Western China, and the chief representatives of it are the Shans and the Karens. According to Mr Taw Sein Ko, the Superintendent of the Archæological Survey, the Shans came from Yunnan, and the Karens from Kueichou. Of the early history of the latter little is known. In the struggles for the supremacy which raged throughout the centuries, from the dawn of history to the advent of the British, they are scarcely mentioned. Father Nerini, a Catholic missionary who was in Burma about the year 1740 A.D., mentions that they had then been settled in the country for generations, but were looked on as savages. They are divided into several tribes, and are scattered all along the sea-board belt from Mergui and Tavoy to Maulmain, and thence, with only a single break near Rangoon, along the delta of the Irrawaddy, up to Cape Negrais, on the border of Arakan. Another tribe occupied the great central range of hills called the Pegu Yoma. They are still almost the sole settlers in these hills, but they have spilt over the plains immediately below, and now occupy the hills and jungles of the Irrawaddy district, and large parts of the Shwegyin, Prome, and Henzada districts. These two branches of the race were persecuted by the Burmese, from whom they hid as much as possible in the hills and in dense jungle. Mr Smeaton, in his " Loyal Karens of Burma," suggests that the tribe on the sea-board between Mergui and Maulmain may have been carried off by invading Siamese. But there is a third branch occupying the hills beyond Toungoo. They are the boldest and most war-like of the Karens, and they succeeded by desperate struggles in resisting Burmese aggression and maintaining their independence. They are known as the Karenni, or Red Karens. Before the annexation of Upper Burma, their little mountain territory lay on the north-east of what was then British Burma, and they paid a small annual tribute to the British Government for the guarantee against aggression which had been given to them.

Although quite out of the struggle for supremacy in historical times, the Karens are a singularly interesting race. Though ignorant of letters, they have preserved what they call the " Traditions of the Elders," which, in parts, at least, seem to imply some Biblical teaching in the remote past. In these it is reiterated that God is unchangeable, eternal, and omnipotent; that He created Heaven and earth, the sun, moon and stars; also man from the earth, and woman from a rib taken from the man. There is also an account of the temptation and fall of man. Mr Smeaton suggests that this was derived from a colony of Jews settled in Western China, and that from the same source came their expectation of the Messiah, and of the roll of parchment to be brought to them by the white foreigners. " Because God cursed us, we are in our present afflicted state, and have no books. But God will again have mercy on us, and again He will love us above others. God will yet

ENTRANCE TO KAREN MOUNTAIN VILLAGE
OF PANGABIN IN THARRAWADDY DISTRICT,
SHOWING BAMBOO STOCKADE

Photograph by Rev. H. I. Marshall, American Baptist Mission, Tharrawaddy

save us again ; it is on account of our listening to the language of Satan, that we thus suffer." It is difficult to believe in anything but a Jewish source for all these ideas, but exactly how and when the Karens thus took up the cry of captive Israel it is impossible to determine. Their features absolutely exclude any idea of Jewish blood, so Mr Smeaton may be correct in attributing it to the influence of a Jewish colony in Western China. Of course, the possession of such ideas immensely facilitated their conversion to Christianity, and the American Baptist Mission has done most noble work among them. Mr Judson, the pioneer in Burma of this Mission, arrived in Maulmain in 1813, and the work which he and his successors have done among the Karens is probably unique in missionary enterprise. They found them hunted savages who would not face a Burman. They have made them a nation of men, civilised, clean-living and brave. In the troublous years succeeding the annexation of Upper Burma in 1886, when the country was seething with dacoity, the Karens came forward and did excellent work in hunting down the dacoits, and restoring order throughout the country. The work was done too, with but scant encouragement from Government. It is true that the Karens knew that their own safety hinged on preserving British rule, but all the same, it was a splendid piece of work they did, and it is all the more remarkable as it was done, not by the Red Karens, who had always maintained their independence, but by the other tribes, who, little more than half-a-century earlier, had been accustomed to fly at sight of a Burman. It is from these down-trodden tribes that the Christian converts have been mainly recruited. Even those who have no sympathy with missionary work must acknowledge that, in this instance at least, it has been amply justified by the results.

The Shan, or Tai race is, undoubtedly, by far the most numerous and the most widely distributed of all the races of Indo-China. It is to be found from Assam to far into the Chinese province of Kwang-Si, and from Bangkok to the interior of Yunnan. Although reckoned as having migrated into what is now known as Burma, after the migration of the Mon-Khmer stock, this must not be taken too literally. Parts of the modern Shan States lie so near Yunnan, the original home of the race, that there may easily have been migrations into that part of the country long before the later migrations which eventually carried the race to Bangkok. This race has had the misfortune to be split up into numerous branches, bearing many different names, speaking many mutually unintelligible languages, and having different written characters, the net result being very confusing. For instance, Siamese gentlemen have found that with patience they can understand their most remote relatives the Hkamti Shans, but they cannot carry on a conversation with their nearest relatives, the Lao. Moreover, though the Siamese language and that of the Hkamti Shans are near enough still to make conversation possible, though difficult, the written characters of these two are the most divergent of any.

It is possible that when such old records as exist in these various languages have been deciphered and studied by competent scholars, much light may be thrown on the ancient history of the race, but, meantime, very little has been done in this direction. Siam is the only independent Tai state in existence, and it has long been the most civilised and advanced. One would naturally expect that Siamese records would furnish the best history of the race, but it is precisely from Siam that no help is to be obtained. Bishop Pallegoix places the commencement of the Shan kingdom of Siam in the middle of the fourteenth century, and previous to that comparatively modern time, there is nothing in Siamese records that can be accepted as history, nothing but fabulous tales which do not even correspond with the legends of the other branches of the race.

Yunnan was not conquered by the Chinese until the year 1253, A.D., when that conquest was achieved by Kublai Khan. Previous to that time there must have been one or more powerful Shan States in Yunnan, or even in Burma itself. Burmese history is not very reliable, but it records two great military expeditions into Burma by "Tayôks," the name now applied to the Chinese. One is said to have occurred shortly before the dawn of the Christian era, and the other nearly three centuries later. This is not likely to be pure invention, but the invaders could not have been Chinese, as these could scarcely have invaded Burma before they had conquered Yunnan. The invaders must have been Shans, the name, "Tayôk," being transferred to the Chinese centuries later, when the Burmese came in contact with them. The spilling over from the kingdom or kingdoms of Yunnan probably began fully two thousand years ago. Some of the migrations were, no doubt, war-like expeditions, such as that which destroyed the pre-historic Burmese kingdom at Tagaung. If the chronicles of the Northern Shans are to be trusted, however, as to dates, the myths recorded in them of the foundation of Shan States in Burma, point to the sixth century as the period of migration. The probability is that the earlier ones were war-like expeditions chiefly, some of which may have permanently settled in Burma. In the sixth century, either from over-population in Yunnan, or from some other cause, the number of such expeditions increased, and the tendency to settle in any conquered territory became more marked. Eventually they spread over the present Shan States, and pushed their way into Assam. The conquest of Yunnan by Kublai Khan, in the thirteenth century, would give a great impetus to this migration, and it was not till after that that the Siamese Tai established themselves in the great delta of the Menam, between Cambodia and the Mon country. It was just about a century after Kublai Khan's conquest of Yunnan that the kingdom of Siam came into being.

After the first incursions of Shans, but long before these immigrants pushed their way down to Siam, the migration of the Tibeto-Burman tribes began. According to Mr Taw Sein Ko, the Chins were the first of these to come, while the Marus, Zis, and Lashis of the Kachin Hills came later. The new-comers migrated into Burma from Eastern Tibet, where the allied tribes, the Lolos and Sifanas, are still to be found. Apparently all the new-comers were rude barbarians, but at a very early period some of them seem to have been organised into a fairly powerful and comparatively civilised state, under the guidance of immigrants from Assam or Gangetic India. The capital of this first Burmese kingdom was at Tagaung on the Irrawaddy. This much seems fairly certain, but the date of this kingdom is very uncertain. According to Burmese annals, Tagaung was founded in the ninth century before Christ, by an Aryan prince from Northern India named Abhiraja. Fifty kings are named as having succeeded him, but even Burmese historians have not attempted to give the dates for these kings, though they have supplied a name for each. The dates would, of course, have been as worthless as the names, had they taken the trouble to supply them. Seeing that even in much later times Burmese historians were much more intent on magnifying the country and its rulers than on recording the exact truth, these early histories may be dismissed as quite worthless. The writers were anxious to exalt the lineage of their kings by connecting them with the Solar and Sakya dynasties of India, an attempt about as futile as it would be to connect the royal house of any European country with the Jewish King David. As to dates, too, the real date being unknown, it was well to give a hoary antiquity to the beginnings of Burmese history.

The date may be utterly disregarded, but at some date, long before the opening of genuine Burmese history, there was some such settlement as that ascribed to Abhiraja. It is further said that when he died, he bequeathed his kingdom to his younger son, while the elder moved to the Chindwin Valley, established his son as King at Kalé there, and then crossing over to Kyaukpadaung, established himself as the first ruler of Arakan. All we can really gather from this is that the first Burmese State seems to have stretched from Tagaung, on the Irrawaddy, to Kyaukpadaung in Arakan. Later it split into two, and Tagaung being overshadowed by powerful Shan States, had always a precarious existence and was eventually overthrown. Arakan, on the other hand, having no formidable neighbours so near, grew in power. According to the Burmese chronicles, after Tagaung was destroyed, the survivors went to Prome, and founded a new settlement there in 483, B.C. Their leader married the Queen of a neighbouring State, supposed to be Burmese, but the Queen's name is unmistakably Shan. From this time onwards, dates as well as names are assigned to the kings who are supposed to have ruled, but both names and dates are of very doubtful authenticity, and would be of little interest even if they could be trusted.

The capital is changed more than once, and occasionally a usurper seizes the throne. Arakan has a similar list of kings, and the Arakanese chroniclers have totally eclipsed those of the Burmese by putting back their first king to the year 2666, B.C. The only point of interest in their chronicle is that they put the accession of their first Buddhist king in the year 146, A.D. As the date of the introduction of Buddhism into Burma is unknown, this date is interesting, though it is too untrustworthy to be taken as really settling the point. The Arakanese speak the same language as the Burmese, though with some differences, and there can be little doubt about their being substantially of the same stock.

When we get to anything like genuine history, and that is not until the seventh century of the Christian era, we find that the various immigrant races had settled down in much the same parts of the country as they occupy at the present day. The Talaings occupied Pegu, and Tenasserim; the Shans were in possession of the Shan States; and the Burmese held the upper portion of the Irrawaddy valley as well as Arakan. Various branches of these same races had got shut up in mountainous or otherwise isolated tracts, and were the ancestors of the numerous more or less wild tribes, Karens, Chins, Kachins, Was, and many others, still to be found in the country. These tribes, however, take little or no part in the subsequent history. They were practically out of the running, and from the dawn of genuine history, in the seventh century, until the advent of the British, early in the nineteenth, the history of the country is a struggle for supremacy between the three dominant races, Talaing, Shan and Burmese. There were incessant wars between them. Now one and then another would inflict a crushing defeat on a rival race, kill great numbers of them, and carry off thousands, often including the royal family, to be slaves in the territory of their conquerors. After a time, the crushed race would rise in rebellion, and, perhaps, retaliate on their former conquerors, putting thousands of them to death, and reducing thousands more to slavery. It was a triangular contest, waged with particular ruthlessness on all sides for over a thousand years, but never reaching any finality. It produced but little beyond a kaleidoscopic shifting of the boundaries of the territory ruled by each race. An energetic warrior king occasionally brought nearly the whole of modern Burma and parts of Siam into nominal subjection to him, and the subject races then had a very hard time of it ; but this never lasted for long. Under his less able successor the yoke would be thrown off, and conquered and conqueror change places.

The introduction of Buddhism into Burma has affected its history so profoundly that it is necessary to consider this before going on to the actual history. Though China may have exerted some influence on the intellectual development of Burma, there can be little doubt that the earliest influences came from India. An active propagandism was started by the Buddhist Church of India some centuries before the dawn of the Christian era, and the adjacent land of Burma would certainly be one of the very first foreign fields to be taken in hand by the Buddhist missionaries. In the middle of the first century after Christ, Buddhism, with its Scriptures in Sanskrit, was introduced into China, and by the fourth century nine-tenths of the inhabitants of China are said to have been Buddhists. Later on, Buddhist and Hindu ideas were alternately accepted and persecuted in China. Burma was not only much nearer to India than China was, but, in the absence of any religion beyond a crude spirit worship, it offered a far more promising field to the apostles of a purer creed. Buddhist missionaries must have been in the country long before the Christian era began, and, though the process of conversion may have been slow, and the conversion often incomplete, the probability is that Buddhism had been accepted by the leading races long before the time of Buddhaghosa, its reputed apostle in Burma. Talaing historians claim him as a fellow-countryman, and say that he went to Ceylon in 402, A.D., and brought back a complete set of the Tripitaka together with its commentaries. This is of very doubtful authenticity as to its details, but Buddhaghosa did live about that time, and if he, or anyone else, left the Talaing country early in the fifth century in search of the Buddhist scriptures, that points to a considerable interest being felt in the country in Buddhist doctrine. The date given by the Arakanese chroniclers to their first Buddhist king may be approximately correct, and by the beginning of the fifth century, Buddhism had probably been adopted by the leading races. In this, as in other matters, the more backward and isolated communities remained out of the main stream of national life, and many of them are still unconverted to Buddhism.

The Talaing story of Buddhaghosa points to a keen interest in Buddhism, by the beginning of the fifth century, among the Talaings. The Arakanese annals put their first Buddhist king in the second century; and the Burmese annals report a falling away into Naga worship at the beginning of the sixth century. But little is known about this heresy, except that its priests called themselves Aris, and that they were not strict observers of their vow of celibacy. Moreover, the basis of their doctrine was that sin could be expiated by the recitation of certain hymns, a doctrine utterly opposed to the teaching of orthodox Buddhism. This heresy seems to have held its ground, among the Burmese at least, for about five centuries; but the point to be considered here is that if the introduction of a heresy is thought of sufficient importance to be chronicled early in the sixth century, the inference is that something approaching orthodox Buddhism had been the accepted religion among the Burmese for a considerable time—possibly for centuries—before. It is uncertain how far this heresy supplanted Buddhism even during its continuance. The two probably existed side by side. Any way, orthodox Buddhism was not forgotten, and when Anawrata, a zealous Buddhist, ascended the throne in 1010, A.D. he had no difficulty in finally stamping out the heresy.

In the early centuries of the Christian era, and probably for some centuries before, Indian traders came to the country as well as Buddhist missionaries. Naturally the Talaings and Arakanese, being on the sea-coast, would see more of both traders and missionaries than the Shans, or the Burmese on the upper reaches of the Irrawaddy. But the civilising influences from India seem to have reached the Burmese of Upper Burma overland, though a long and difficult overland journey must have rendered such influence less frequent than in the case of the dwellers on the coast. Both the Burmese and the Talaings, however, seem to have looked to India for knowledge, and it was well for them that they did so just at the time when the Buddhist propagandism was most active. It is owing to that fact that they have escaped entirely the caste system and all that it involves. The Shans, no doubt, though they may have got their religion from Indian missionaries, were but little thrown in contact with the Indian traders. But the Shans may have brought a higher civilisation with them from Yunnan than the other immigrant races had brought from their homes ; and, through Yunnan, they probably remained more or less in touch with Chinese civilisation, though Yunnan was independent until its conquest by Kublai Khan in the thirteenth century.

CHAPTER II.

A.D. 639 TO 1010

THE commencement of the era now in general use among the chief races inhabiting Burma may be taken as the period at which something like genuine history commences. But little is known, however, of the causes which led to the introduction of that era. It is spoken of by some authorities as having been introduced in the year 638 A.D., while others assign it to 639. If we subtract the current Burmese year from the current Christian one, we get the result 638 or 639 according to the time of year at which the calculation is made. For instance, any time between the 1st January and 14th April, 1908, the deduction of 1269, the current Burmese year, from 1908 would have given 639 as the result; but on 15th April, the Burmese new year, 1270, began, and from that time on till the close of 1908, the deduction would leave 638. The Burmese chronicles give no reason for the introduction of a new era, but they ascribe it to a king named Thinga Raja, or Popa Saw Rahan, a usurper, who had been a monk, and the Preceptor of the Queen of his predecessor. On the death of the preceding king, the monk became a layman again, which a Buddhist monk is always entitled to do, and married the widowed Queen. Although he is credited with having introduced the new calendar, according to the dates given in the Burmese chronicles, his successor ascended the throne in 637 A.D., that is, a year before the new era began.

Authorities seem to be agreed that the new era was based on astronomical calculations, and commenced on the day in which the sun is supposed to enter the first sign of the zodiac. According to Garnier, who is quoted as an authority by Forbes, in his " Languages of Further India," and again by Mr Taw Sein Ko :—"On 21st March, 638, the new moon coincided with the entry of the sun into the first sign of the zodiac, and produced an important eclipse." But on the point of the origin of the era, the authorities are divided. Phayre says that the Burmese system of astronomy and method of computing time are essentially those of the Hindus. Parker, too, speaks of the Burmese computation of time being essentially Hindu, and the new era Hindu handiwork. But Forbes speaks of the " singular fact that all the nations of ultra-India, although deriving their religion, their civilisation and their literature from India, have not adopted any of the Indian eras, but have borrowed from China." Garnier, too, speaks of the astronomical knowledge of the Chinese as the possible origin of the era now in use in Burma, and the adjoining countries. Mr Taw Sein Ko also leans to the idea of a Chinese origin.

Whether the era came from India or from China, it was very generally adopted, and has held its ground ever since. Thinga Raja gets the credit of its introduction, and probably did do so, the date given to his successor being a mistake. Burmese chroniclers were not very particular about dates. There is some reason to think that Thinga Raja was not only a usurper, but of Shan origin, or possibly Cambodian. He seems to have been a man of some ability, however, and is said to have introduced many improvements into the administration. But there is very little known about him, or what his reforms, beyond that of the calendar, really were. Long before his time—early in the second century, A.D., according to the chronicles—the capital of the Burmese nation had been shifted to Pagan. Tagaung, the pre-historic capital, is also called Pagan, or Old Pagan, sometimes, and the two must not be confounded. Tagaung, or Old Pagan, is between Mandalay and Bhamo. New Pagan, the only Pagan that attained to greatness, lies as far south of Mandalay as the other is north of it. Tagaung, or Old Pagan, was overthrown long before the dawn of history. One or more capitals succeeded it before New Pagan was founded.

In Thinga Raja's time, New Pagan was an insignificant place, and the territory which he ruled could not have been very extensive. Arakan had its own king, and the Talaing kingdom in Pegu and Tenasserim was too powerful for the Burmese of the Upper Irrawaddy to interfere with. It was all they could do to hold their own against the powerful Shan States in their neighbourhood. Had these Shan States coalesced under one powerful monarch, the Burmese of Upper Burma would not have been able to stand against them. In spite of the advantage of possessing territory on both sides of a navigable river, and numerous States instead of one powerful one for their immediate neighbours, the Burmese were occasionally overwhelmed by the Shans and had to submit to the rule of Shan kings. Thinga Raja, himself, was probably a Shan. At that time, too, the Talaings were, not only far more powerful than the Burmese, but more advanced in civilisation, so had they advanced on Upper Burma they would have conquered it. But the Talaings, being in possession of the rich delta of the Irrawaddy and of Tenasserim, both blessed with an abundant rainfall, had no inducement to venture into the comparatively arid country of Upper Burma. Under these circumstances, the Burmese were able to maintain their footing and to become consolidated into a nation.

The mere record of the kings who succeeded Thinga Raja would be of no interest, but Mr Parker gives an interesting extract from the chapter on " Southern Barbarians," in the T'ang history, which throws a much clearer light on the Burma of the eighth and ninth centuries than the Burmese annals do. It shows how they impressed a contemporary Chinaman, though he, of course, despised them as barbarians. He calls them " Piao," and says that when the king goes out in his palankeen, he reposes on a couch of golden cord ; but for long distances he rides an elephant. " They dislike taking life. They greet each other by embracing the arm with the hand. They know how to make astronomical calculations, and are devotees of Buddhism. They have a hundred monasteries with bricks of vitreous ware, embellished with gold and silver, vermilion, gay colours and red kino. The floor is painted and covered with ornamented carpets. The king's residence is in like style. The people cut their hair at seven years of age and enter a monastery. If at the age of twenty they have not grasped the doctrine, they become lay people again. For clothes they wear a cotton *sarang*, holding that, as silk involves the taking of life, it ought not to be worn. On the head they wear golden-flowered hats with a blue net, or bag set with pearls. In the king's palace there are placed two bells, one of gold and one of silver ; when an enemy comes they burn incense and beat the bells, in order to divine their good or evil fortune. There is a huge white elephant a hundred feet high ; litigants burn incense and kneel before the elephant, reflecting within themselves whether they are right or wrong, after which they retire. When there is any disaster or plague, the

A BUDDHIST MONASTERY

Photograph by Mr P. Klier, Rangoon

King also kneels down in front of the elephant and blames himself. . . . The women twist their hair high up on the crown of the head, and ornament it with strings of pearls; they wear a natural-tinted female petticoat, and throw pieces of delicate silk over themselves. When walking they hold a fan, and the wives of exalted persons have four or five individuals at each side holding fans. . . . Nan-chao used to exercise suzerainty over it on account of its contiguity, and by reason of the military strength of Nan-chao. Towards the close of the eighth century A.D., the King Yung K'iang, hearing that Nan-chao had become part of the T'ang Empire, had a desire to join China too, and Imousün sent an envoy named Yang Kia-ming to Kien-nan. The Viceroy of Si-ch'wan, Wei Kao, begged permission to offer the Emperor some barbarian songs, and, moreover, told the Piao State to send up some musicians. For specimens of their music see the General Annals. His Majesty Divus Têh made Shu-nan-do President of the Imperial Mews, and sent him back. The Governor of K'ai Chou submitted a panegyric upon the Piao music. In the year 832 the Nan-chao monarch kidnapped three thousand Burmans, and colonised his newly acquired eastern dominions with them."

This extract shows that life in Burma in the ninth century of the Christian era was very similar in many ways to what it continued to be under the Burmese kings until nearly the close of the nineteenth century. There was considerable luxury of a primitive kind, in the palace at least, which was built in the same style as the monasteries, of which there were a great number. No mention is made of pagodas, but the pagodas of the time were probably insignificant structures, as the Burmese first learned to build imposing pagodas from captive Talaings in the eleventh century. In the ninth century they could make astronomical calculations, but we are not told whether this knowledge came from India or from China. They were devotees of Buddhism, and the boys all entered a monastery at an early age and stayed there for a number of years. Burma has had, for a thousand years at least, possibly for much longer, a system of free, and practically universal education for its sons. It is doubtful whether any other country can compare with it in this respect. The education may not have amounted to much from the secular point of view. The object of it was not to give secular knowledge, or to help a lad to get on in life, but to teach him the vanity of all earthly things, and to set his feet on the path of renunciation, which alone leads to peace. The successful scholars, from the point of view of the monks, were those who "grasped the doctrine," and became monks. Those who became lay people again on attaining manhood were failures, who went back to the vanities of life, and so increased the number of weary lives they would have to go through before attaining Nirvana. The dimly understood metaphysical subtleties which had been their mental food in the monastery, were a poor preparation for the battle of life. But they had at least learned to read and write, and had acquired some elementary arithmetic, so had more secular knowledge than fell to the lot of their contemporaries in other countries.

It is somewhat curious that, with the general diffusion of even elementary education going on century after century, the Burmese should never have made any progress in the arts of life. But, to any one who knows from experience what life was in Upper Burma in the times of the later kings, the reason is obvious. Under such a crushing despotism no progress was possible.

The King's caprice was law, and against him no one had any rights at all. Remoteness from the capital or obscurity in it might secure immunity from the personal notice of the King himself, but his officials were everywhere, and it was impossible to escape their notice if one did anything out of the common. So long as the officials paid into the King's treasury the contributions expected from their districts, they could tyrannise over the unfortunate people as they pleased. If a man's wife, sister, or daughter, took the fancy of an official, she had to be given up to him. Any sign of wealth was the surest way to invite attention and torture until it was all surrendered. In fact the truest wisdom, in such a community, lay in producing just enough to keep one's family alive, and courting obscurity as much as possible. The bolder spirits aimed at becoming officials, but, though a certain amount of comparative wealth was then possible, the official's head was never very secure on his shoulders. A hint to the King that he was appropriating an undue share of the revenue he raised might lead at any time to his degradation and death. Dacoity was another outlet for the bolder spirits, and it was less dangerous, perhaps, than official life, but less lucrative also. The man who wished a quiet life could find it only in poverty, either in or out of a monastery. The scholar would naturally be attracted to the monastery. He was safer there than anywhere else; his food and shelter were secure; and he could study to his heart's content. But no literature was available except interminable discourses on Buddhist doctrine and preposterous religious tales in illustration of it. In spite of the tolerance of Buddhism, it was almost impossible for any one to break out of the net-work of metaphysical subtleties which constituted the intellectual environment of the nation, and to make any start towards real knowledge. With the exception of the drama, perhaps, no advance was made throughout the centuries, in spite of practically universal elementary education among the men. Generation succeeded generation, and century succeeded century, with the barren result that the intellect of the nation was absorbed continuously in spinning intellectual cobwebs, while science remained unborn.

To return, however, to the Chinese account of Burma in the ninth century, the men of that time, apparently, objected to wearing silk, as that involves the taking of life. The women, on the other hand, were not so conscientious, as they threw pieces of delicate silk over themselves, much as they do now. The men have, of course, long followed suit in this respect, and wear silk without scruple. It seems unlikely that the objection on the part of the men was quite so universal even in the ninth century, as is represented. The Burmese woman had, evidently, a great deal of freedom even then, as she has always had and has still; but it seems improbable that she would have defied the whole male conscience of the nation, more especially the conscience of the venerated monks, had the male conscience been entirely opposed to the use of silk. It is difficult to judge, however, as dress is precisely the subject on which women all the world over are least amenable to reason as it appears to men, even to the venerated clergy.

The account of the huge white elephant, a hundred feet high, is curious. Mr Parker expresses some doubt as to whether "image" or "elephant" is meant; the two words being identical in sound. Whichever it was, the proceedings in regard to it scarcely conform to strict Buddhist orthodoxy, but various heterodox customs still prevail among the Burmese, and the Buddhism of the ninth century was admittedly corrupt. Mr Taw Sein Ko says:—"Burmese records relate that, prior to the eleventh century, offerings of wine and meat were made to images of Buddha; and that it was only in 1555 A.D., that the Hanthawadi Sinbyuyin, the Branginoco of the early European writers, ordered the cessation of the practice of offering to the Nats or deified spirits intoxicants and sacrifices of white buffaloes, white oxen, and white goats. That the Tantric doctrines became part and parcel of the prevailing system of faith in Burma, is further shewn by the fact that, even at the present day, Nat-worship is not wholly free from licentiousness."

It is evident that the Shans had exercised suzerainty over Upper Burma in earlier times, but by the ninth century this had been shaken off to some extent, though then the Nan-chao monarch could still make his power felt, even to the extent of kidnapping three thousand Burmans when he wanted them. Mr Parker's comments on the reference to Nan-chao are as follows:—"Imousün was the most in evidence if not the most distinguished of the Nan-chao kings. Kien-nan and K'aichou were both in Sz-ch'wan, or Si-ch'wan, as part of it was then called. Shu-nando, we are told elsewhere, was the King's heir, and as *nandaw* means 'palace' in modern Burmese, it seems not improbable that there may be some attempt in the tri-syllabic word to translate the Chinese words *tung-kung* or 'eastern palace' meaning 'heir-apparent.' Governor Sü Kiyu's Geography states that the envoy on this occasion was one Sih-li-i, the King's younger brother, so that it is all the more likely that Shunando is not a personal name. Chinese history tells us that Imousün's father annexed the dominions of the Pyü, and that his son styled himself *Piao-sin*. This word suggests the Burmese *Pyu-Sheng*, or 'King of the

Pyü,' just as some of the modern Kings styled themselves *Hseng-byu-sheng*, or 'lords of the white elephant.' Any way it is abundantly clear that during the ninth century, Burma, whatever its size may have been, was, at least so far as its northern portion was concerned, inferior in power to the Shan kingdom of modern Tali-fu, which at one time came very nearly overthrowing the Chinese T'ang dynasty."

Very little more is known of the history of Burma up to the close of the tenth century. In Upper Burma the contest with the Shans continued with varying success, and in religion, the Tantric system, with its immoral professors, the Aris, and the form of Naga-worship, continued to exist side by side with a Buddhism of somewhat doubtful orthodoxy. In Arakan and in the Talaing country there were religious troubles too, but springing from a different source. There the struggle was between the Brahmins and the Buddhists, Indian influences being still predominant all along the sea-coast. Fortunately for Burma the Buddhists carried the day, but, though we know the final issue of the struggle, the details have all been lost. The lists of kings who ruled in Arakan and the Talaing country during these centuries are of no interest to anyone, though they may be fairly correct, at least in comparison with the earlier lists, which, in the case of Arakan, profess to take us back to 2666 B.C.

CHAPTER III.

A.D. 1010 TO 1298

THE eleventh century brought about a great change in the relative positions of the three races which struggled for supremacy in the country. In the year 1010 A.D., Anawrata ascended the throne at Pagan. He was a man of character and determination, who set himself with ardour, both to the reform of religion and to extending the boundaries of his kingdom. In regard to religion he seems to have known that the form of Buddhism then prevailing in Upper Burma was corrupt, but he did not know exactly what the true doctrine should be. While he was looking for light, a Talaing missionary arrived from Thaton, the Talaing capital, and expounded religion to the people at Pagan. He had come, he said, because he had heard that the true religion was not known in Pagan. The king sent for him and listened gladly to his message. Here was the guidance he wanted, and he became a zealous convert. The false Aris were expelled from the monasteries, and their places were filled by orthodox monks brought from Thaton. The people seem to have acquiesced in this reform, and the orthodoxy established by Anawrata has held its ground to the present day. Even yet, of course, there are vestiges of the old pre-Buddhistic Nat-worship in the practices of the people, but theoretically they are all Buddhists, orthodox according to the standard laid down in the eleventh century by the teachers imported from Thaton, and since Anawrata's time there has been little or no conscious heresy. The vestiges of Nat-worship which still exist can scarcely be called conscious heresy. Though they are not strictly in accord with Buddhist doctrine, it is doubtful whether the people realise that. In fact, they are simply a survival of very old customs, the non-Buddhistic origin of which has been wholly lost sight of. A layman may easily practice them and yet believe himself to be an orthodox Buddhist.

In addition to his thorough reform of religion, King Anawrata carried on an extensive system of conquest. He broke the power of the Shan States in his immediate neighbourhood, wrested from them lands they had seized from the Burmese, and established some sort of supremacy over the nearest Shan States. According to Sir Arthur Phayre, individual states of Shan chiefs in the Upper Irrawaddy, still retained independent power ; but from this time those to the south of Bhamo were more or less subordinate to the Burmese monarchy. Further, Anawrata seems to have established an ascendancy, though of a less permanent character, over Arakan. He is said to have made a progress as far as Bengal, though this seems somewhat unlikely. With the Shans still more or less unsubdued, and apt to give trouble near the capital, it would have been risky for the King to be absent for the length of time that a difficult land journey from Pagan to the borders of Bengal would have involved. That he did invade Arakan, however, is admitted even by the Arakanese chroniclers. They add that the Shans had invaded Arakan eighteen years before, and had proved themselves hard masters, robbing the people and plundering the pagodas. It was when they retired, that Anawrata's invasion took place, according to the Arakanese chronicles. His object is stated to have been to obtain possession of a famous image of Buddha, which was greatly venerated by the Arakanese. It was only owing to " supernatural interposition " that he was prevented from carrying away this image. Indirectly, this is an admission by the Arakanese that they were quite unable at that time to cope with the Burmese. As an instance of the utterly untrustworthy nature of the dates in these chronicles, it may be mentioned that the Arakanese chronicles place Anawrata's invasion in the year 995 A.D., whereas, according to the Burmese chronicle, his accession took place in 1010 A.D., and his conversion to orthodox Buddhism came after his accession. He might, possibly, have been sent to invade Arakan before his accession to the throne, but his object then could scarcely have been the sacred image.

Anawrata's religious zeal led him to make war on the Talaings. This showed a want of gratitude to the people who had given him the gift of truth, which, as a Buddhist, he should have regarded as above all other gifts. His whole method of dealing with the Talaings in this unhappy war showed, moreover, that in spite of all his zeal for religion, he had caught nothing of its inner meaning or of the spirit of its founder. It was not an image he wanted from the Talaings, but the Buddhist Scriptures, the Tripitaka. A copy of these existed in Thaton, so he sent an ambassador to ask for a copy. According to the Burmese chronicle, the Talaing King answered haughtily that he would give nothing. According to a tradition preserved among the Taungthus, a tribe scattered over parts of Burma, Siam and Cambodia, the Talaing King's answer to Anawrata was insulting enough to exasperate anyone. It was to the effect that the subjects of the King of Pagan were so exceedingly ignorant and wild that a copy of the Scriptures would be wasted on them, as they would not be able to understand it. The haughty answer of the Talaing King, whether or not it took the insulting form preserved in Taungthu tradition, was destined to bring on him a very heavy punishment. King Anawrata was naturally very angry, so he collected a large army and went down the Irrawaddy. Apparently no attempt was made to meet the invaders on the way, but the Talaing capital was surrounded by a wall, and a stout resistance was made there. The Burmese army, however, surrounded the city, and after a long siege, famine compelled the people of Thaton to surrender. The city was utterly destroyed, the records perished, and King Anawrata took not only the sacred books, but images, relics, and treasures of all sorts, away to Pagan. The Talaing King, his wives and children, also the leading Talaings were taken as captives to the Burmese capital, and there degraded to the position of pagoda slaves. Artificers and scholars were also carried off in numbers, but their lot was happier, as they were not reduced to the absolutely hopeless position of pagoda slaves. They lost their liberty, no doubt, but their work was to teach the Burmese what they knew, more especially pagoda building, and in time their children would be free, even if the original captives did not attain freedom in their own lifetime.

It was a crushing defeat that Anawrata inflicted on the Talaings, and it is no wonder that he is the great hero of the Burmese people. When he ascended the throne at Pagan, his rule extended over a limited area only, on either side of the Upper Irrawaddy. The Shan States in the neighbourhood were quite independent, and, at times, were inclined to oppress the Burmese. Anawrata altered all this, won back territory that had been taken by the Shans, reduced some Shan States to vassalage, and altogether changed the relative positions of Shan and Burman. By extending his sway over Arakan and the Talaing country also, he brought under one rule, for the first time, an extent of country corresponding very much to modern Burma. In those days of imperfect communications, his rule over the outlying parts of his empire amounted, no doubt, to little more than the exaction of tribute, but his supremacy was acknowledged throughout the country now known as Burma, excepting the Shan States which lie at a considerable distance from the Irrawaddy.

Having obtained everything he wanted from the Talaings, King Anawrata next set his heart on obtaining a tooth of Buddha, which had been imported into China some centuries earlier. This, however, was a larger order than taking the Tripitaka from the Talaings. Not only was China more powerful than the Talaing kingdom, but it was more remote, and Yunnan, which was still independent of China, had to be passed through. The Burmese chronicles record a meeting between the Burmese King and the Emperor of China, and add that though the former did not get the tooth he wanted, he brought away a golden image which had been sanctified by direct contact with the holy tooth. This, however, is pure invention. It is certain that Anawrata never got further than a part of Yunnan, called in the Burmese chronicles Gundalarît, and never met the Emperor of China at all. If he got a golden image it must have been one from the Shan States, and one that had probably never been near the sacred tooth. He did, however, bring home a new wife. According to Sir Arthur Phayre, " on his return to his own kingdom, while passing through the Shan State of Moa, he married the daughter of the chief ; and the romantic events which led to the marriage, together with the trials through which the bride passed, and her final triumphs over the plots of jealous rivals, are represented in a drama which is one of the most popular on the Burmese stage."

King Anawrata made yet two other attempts to procure holy relics for Pagan. A forehead bone of Buddha was said to be enshrined in a pagoda near Prome, so he demolished this pagoda in order to bring this relic to be deposited in the Shwezigon pagoda which he was building at Pagan. Here, too, he was disappointed, as, "in consequence of the sin he had committed in destroying the original pagoda, or from some other hidden cause," that holy relic had disappeared. He then sent to Ceylon to try and obtain the famous tooth-relic enshrined there, but was forced to content himself with what was said to be a miraculous emanation from the holy tooth.

To us in the twentieth century, these quests of holy relics seem simply ridiculous, but in the eleventh century men everywhere looked at them from a totally different point of view. King Anawrata's energy in trying to obtain them shows the man's character. He was equally energetic in what we consider more practical directions, as is proved by the way in which he extended his empire. Burma has seen few kings as capable as he, and his figure stands out more prominently, in spite of the lapse of centuries, than that of any other king who has ever ruled in the country. According to the Burmese chronicle he reigned for forty-two years, and, died in the year 1052 A.D.

The immediate successors of Anawrata seem to have been fairly capable, and to have maintained the supremacy in the country which he had won. The first of them had to put down a rebellion in Pegu, the new capital of the Talaing country, but this rebellion was headed by the Burmese governor, whom the king had appointed, and when he was killed in battle, the Talaing revolt ceased. The crushing defeat they had sustained at the hands of Anawrata had taken the spirit out of them so completely that several generations had to pass before they gathered sufficient courage for a national revolt. Over Arakan the supremacy was less complete. Before the close of the eleventh century, a usurper seized the throne of Arakan, killing the king, who was tributary to Pagan. The son of the murdered king, however, escaped to Pagan, and remained there in exile for twenty-five years. At the end of that time, the reigning king of Pagan, Anawrata's great-grandson, determined to restore the rightful heir to the throne of Arakan. He sent a large army of both Burmese and Talaings, and effected the restoration in the year 1103 A.D., though the usurper made a stubborn resistance. This incident is not mentioned in either the Burmese or the Arakanese chronicles, but is recorded on a stone slab at Buddha Gaya, in connection with repairs to the temple made by the restored king of Arakan, in fulfilment of an engagement he had made with the king of Pagan.

About a century later an invasion of Burma took place which is recorded in the annals of Ceylon, but of which the Burmese chroniclers make no mention. The King of Ceylon was in the habit of maintaining an agent at Pegu. He is called an ambassador, but as his residence was at Pegu, the capital of the conquered Talaing country only, instead of at Pagan, he was probably more of a trading agent than an ambassador. The King of Burma, however, defrayed his expenses, it being the Burmese custom thus to provide for the representatives of foreign powers. Early in the thirteenth century, however, the

King of Burma took it into his head to stop the usual payments, to seize some Singhalese ships, then in Burmese waters, and to commit other offences towards subjects of the King of Ceylon. The latter promptly sent an army to avenge these wrongs; the Burmese were beaten and a tribute of elephants promised. The Singhalese version may somewhat exaggerate the facts, but the complete silence of the Burmese historians proves that the incident scarcely redounded to the credit of Burma. When they could not twist a discreditable incident into a creditable one, they suppressed it altogether.

During the two centuries immediately following the death of Anawrata, the main energies of the Burmese people seem to have been devoted to pagoda building. The ruins of Pagan at the present day prove with what energy this was carried on. No other capital of Burma, either before or after, can have approached the magnificence of Pagan in the day of her greatness. Her ruins are still the most impressive spectacle in the country. If one climbs to the top of one of the pagodas, one sees ruined pagodas in every direction, pagodas of every shape and every size, and there is practically nothing else in sight but these remains of the religious zeal of Anawrata and his successors. Of the secular buildings not a trace remains, though there must have been a very considerable population. The palace of the King, the monasteries of the monks, and the dwellings of the people have all disappeared, leaving not a trace behind. Nothing is left but countless pagodas, ranging from the magnificent Ananda pagoda down to the most ordinary small pagoda, such as is to be found in every Burmese village. The captive Talaings were the first teachers in pagoda building, but there is every reason to believe that help

ANANDA PAGODA, PAGAN

Photograph by Mr Samuels, Mandalay

came also from Southern India and from Ceylon. Even so, however, it is not easy to account for the architecture of some of the finer pagodas still extant. The ground plan of the Ananda pagoda, for instance, is a perfect Greek cross, and in more than one of them, one is strangely reminded of the churches of Southern Catholic Europe. Anawrata began this pagoda building, but he had his hands full of other matters, and did but little in the way of actual building. All the great religious buildings, which make Pagan to-day such a wonderful scene of desolation, were built between 1057 and 1227 A.D. The Ananda pagoda was built by one of Anawrata's sons, who came to the throne in 1057 A.D., so it is one of the earliest as well as one of the most remarkable. The religious zeal which for two centuries kept a whole people so absorbed in building religious edifices is remarkable enough in itself, but it is still more remarkable that in the eleventh century the Burmese should have been able to produce such pagodas as the Ananda. In later times, pagoda building consisted in endless repetitions of the same form, but in the first flush of zeal a diversity of form and an excellence of architectural skill was achieved almost at a bound, and has never been equalled since. As Sir Arthur Phayre says :—" Mr James Fergusson remarks on the almost universal use in them of the pointed arch, not only in the openings, but in the vaulted coverings of the passages, and finds that in no other country of Asia, from the Euphrates to the Ganges, is the existence of such form, in buildings of the period to which they belong, to be met with." It is a pity that so few of those who visit Burma see anything more of Pagan than a distant glimpse of it from the deck of a river steamer. It is in many ways the most interesting sight in the country. The succeeding centuries have produced nothing to equal those relics of the religious enthusiasm which pervaded the nation from the eleventh to the thirteenth century.

In the year 1248 A.D., a king ascended the throne at Pagan who is known in history as "The King who fled from the Chinese." He is said to have lived in greater luxury than any of his predecessors, which may mark some falling off in the religious zeal which had animated them for over two centuries. But he was not to be out-done by them in pagoda building, so he started one which was to exceed them all in costliness, though falling far short of them in architectural design. For a time it had to be stopped, as the country was exhausted, but then he pushed it on again, and it was finally completed in 1274 A.D., the relic-chamber being filled with golden vessels. After that, however, disaster after disaster fell on this King. Early in his reign there had been an insurrection in Martaban. That was put down, but many Shans, from Zimmè and other adjoining states, had settled there, and one of them who had acquired wealth and authority succeeded later in a revolt. He killed the Burmese governor, and made himself King of Martaban. The Talaings at Pegu, also, were becoming very restive under Burmese rule. Many of the Burmese officers there had married Talaing wives, and one of these officers headed a successful revolt against the King of Pagan. A Burmese army was sent against him, but he defeated that, and became King of Pegu. Eventually the rebel Kings of Martaban and of Pegu combined, and forced the Burmese army back to Upper Burma.

Meantime a very much more serious danger was threatening the Pagan Monarchy from another quarter. In 1254 A.D. Kublai Khan conquered the State of Tali, thus bringing the Chinese power into close proximity with Burma. This was followed, some years later, by a demand for tribute from Burma, and there seem to have been some collisions between Burmese and Chinese troops. The Burmese King had also murdered some of the Chinese ambassadors, or messengers, thereby bringing down on his head a more formidable Chinese invasion. A battle was fought in which the Burmese army was hopelessly defeated. On hearing of this defeat, the King hastily left Pagan, thereby earning the nick-name by which he is known in history. Sir Arthur Phayre says that the Mongol army plundered Pagan and penetrated as far south as Taroup-mau, or Chinese point, south of Prome. Mr Parker doubts whether the Chinese army ever got beyond Tagaung, or Old Pagan. But if the Chinese army omitted to plunder Pagan, there would be no lack of others, the neighbouring Shan chiefs for instance, to avail themselves of the opportunity in the general confusion.

The unfortunate Burmese King fled to Bassein, where he found an asylum for five months. The Burmese historian severely condemns the excessive luxury he in dulged in, even then, when his country was ruined. After the five months' stay in Bassein he determined to return to Pagan, but he only reached Prome, where one of his sons was the governor. This prince forced his father to swallow poison. Sir Arthur Phayre gives 1285 A.D. as the date of this, but the Burmese chronicle makes this King's reign end in 1279, and Mr Parker puts the Mongol invasion in 1286 A.D. The last date is probably correct, in which case the King's death would be either in that or in the following yeaı Three of his sons, including the one who had killed his ıather, disputed the succession. One of them, not the parricide, did succeed in placing himself on the throne at Pagan, but the empire had fallen to pieces, and it was only a pitiful remnant of it in which he exercised any authority. Even that he did not keep for any length of time, as he was deposed and killed in 1298 A.D., and with him the Anawrata dynasty came to an end.

CHAPTER IV.

A.D. 1298 TO 1557

EVEN before the total collapse of the Burmese Empire which followed the Mongol invasion, signs of weakness had been apparent. The Talaings had thrown off the Burmese yoke. So, no doubt, had such Shan States as had previously acknowledged the suzerainty of the King of Pagan. In addition to this, men of Shan race had acquired influence in Upper Burma itself. Before the Pagan Empire went down in total eclipse, three Shan brothers had been appointed governors of districts, and it is possible that the General of the Mongol army, before leaving, may have given them some authority to govern the country. He would naturally prefer Shan to Burmese rulers. Whether there was any such authority or not, the Burmese chronicle gives the name of three Shan brothers who began their rule in 1298 A.D. These are, doubtless, the three Shan governors who continued in their governorships as independent Kings. Eventually one brother seems to have amalgamated the three districts into one petty kingdom, which he and his five successors ruled from Panya, which had been the chief town of his own district. This kingdom lasted only from 1298 to 1364. Meantime, in 1315, one of his sons had set up another kingdom, with its capital at Sagaing. This kingdom also came to an end in 1364.

It is evident that throughout this period the Shans ruled Upper Burma. Even the next King, who overthrew these two kingdoms, and founded the city of Ava in 1364, was clearly a Shan. He claimed descent from the ancient Kings of Tagaung, as well as from the first Shan King of Sagaing. The latter claim was, doubtless, genuine enough; the former is manifestly absurd. The King of Sagaing is said to have been driven out by an army of northern Shans. All that can safely be taken out of this is that the Shans were all powerful in Upper Burma from 1298 to 1364, and that the Burmese were utterly crushed during that time. The King who founded Ava, however, seems to have thought it worth while to conciliate the Burmese by claiming descent from the ancient Kings of Tagaung. He could not prove it, of course, but neither could any one else disprove it. His successor went one better and claimed descent from the Pagan Kings, as well as from the three Shan brothers. He is said to have been "elected to the throne" on these grounds, but it is hard to believe that any real election to the throne could have taken place in Burma in the fourteenth century. The ministers who intrigued the succession may have considered that the descent claimed, whether real or not, was a factor worth taking into consideration, as being likely to please both Shans and Burmese. But the Kings who reigned in Ava from 1364 to 1554 were all, undoubtedly, Shans, though some of them found it politic to claim descent also from the Kings of Tagaung or those of Pagan.

While the Shans were thus ruling Upper Burma they were also exerting a considerable influence further south. Even in the time of the King who ran away from the Chinese, a Shan had managed to set himself up as the King of Martaban, and in conjunction with the

GROUP OF SHANS

Photograph by Mr Samuels, Mandalay

rebel King of Pegu had driven back the Burmese army sent to punish them. These two worthies, however, fell out shortly afterwards, fought, and Wareru, the King of Martaban, became King of Pegu also. The Shan brothers ruling in Upper Burma seem to have made no claim to suzerainty over Pegu and Martaban, but they sent an army to try and obtain a white elephant which Wareru had. He was able, however, to defeat this army, which could scarcely have been very considerable, and he was left to reign in peace for the remainder of his life. Pegu and Martaban continued to be ruled by Kings of the Shan race until 1540 A.D., the capital being at Martaban, for about sixty years, after which it was transferred to Pegu.

Thus from the close of the thirteenth to the middle of the sixteenth century, all Burma, except Arakan, was ruled by Kings of the Shan race. With the fatal tendency of that race, however, to split into different small kingdoms, they did not amalgamate into one powerful empire, but remained separate and hostile to each other. The different parts of the country fought with each other just as frequently and as bitterly as if each part had been ruled by a King of its own race. We have seen that the Shan Kings of Upper Burma soon found it politic to claim descent from the old Burmese Kings. The Shan Kings of Lower Burma do not seem to have claimed descent from the Talaing Kings, but, in process of time, no doubt, intermarriage with the people led both royal houses to lose their distinctively Shan nationality. Their titles to their respective thrones, however, rested chiefly on their Shan descent.

Meantime the Shans were also pressing down to Siam. Immediately after Kublai Khan's conquest of Yunnan, the Shans migrated in considerable numbers and formed the States of Laos, Luang Prabang, Vienchau, Zimmè and Siam. The last of these was destined to become the most powerful Shan State, and, though it was not properly consolidated until about the middle of the fourteenth century, we hear of a King of Siam before that. For instance, the King of Martaban, who succeeded Wareru in 1306 A.D., solicited a recognition of his title from the King of Siam, and seems to have acknowledged him as suzerain. In spite of this there were various wars between Wareru's successors and the Kings of Siam, during which Tavoy and Tenasserim changed hands more than once. According to Siamese history, Tenasserim, Tavoy, Martaban and Maulmain were all subject to Siam in 1350 A.D., when the capital, Ayuthia, was founded. The two first named towns may have been, but not the last two at that time.

The Kings of Upper and Lower Burma, not content with invading each other's territory, both interfered in the affairs of Arakan, making that distracted country one of their battle-fields. In 1406 A.D., the King of Arakan was driven out of his country by an army from Upper Burma. He took refuge in Bengal, where he remained in exile for twenty-four years. The King of Burma put his own son-in-law on the throne of Arakan, whereupon the King of Pegu invaded Arakan, killed the King of Burma's nominee, and put his own man on the throne. Thereupon, of course, the King of Burma invaded Pegu, but the King of Pegu's nominee kept the throne of Arakan. In 1430 A.D., however, the King of Bengal determined to restore the exiled King, and did so, the restored King becoming a vassal of Bengal. This vassalage did not continue for long, but from this time the Arakanese Kings used Mahomedan designations in addition to their own names, and even issued coins bearing the Kalima.

All this probably began as a sign of vassalage to the Mahomedan Kings of Bengal, and was continued as a token of sovereignty over Chittagong, which Arakan managed to annex in 1459 A.D.

While the Kings of Upper Burma, of Pegu, and of Arakan were fighting with each other on every possible occasion, to say nothing of Upper Burma's wars with Shan chiefs, Pegu's wars with Siam, and Arakan's annexation of Chittagong; an obscure kingdom, that of Taungu, was rising into some prominence. Taungu lies near the hills occupied by the Karens, and is never mentioned in Burmese history till the twelfth century of the Christian era, when one of Anawrata's successors is said to have visited it. Wareru, the Shan King of Martaban, is also said to have entered it a century later, and to have carried away the chief then ruling. But this chief's two sons established themselves in a stronghold among the hills. After the fall of the Pagan monarchy, the Shan Kings continued to send governors to Taungu, but by the beginning of the fifteenth century the rulers of Taungu were so powerful that the Kings of Ava had to conciliate them. One of them came to Ava when invited in 1406 A.D., and was received with great distinction. This did not conciliate him, however, and shortly afterwards he entered into an alliance with the King of Pegu. They made a joint attack on Prome, then subject, nominally at least, to the King of Burma, but in this they were not successful, apparently. In 1437, the King of Pegu managed to put one of his own sons on the throne of Taungu. After five years the King of Burma managed to turn him out, and put a Shan chief of his own nomination on the throne of Taungu. This man held his own, and was succeeded by his son, but the allegiance of Taungu to Burma was always very doubtful.

Later, the King of Burma sent his foster-brother to rule this troublesome province, but he, too, threw off his allegiance, and induced the King of Pegu to join him in resisting the Burmese army. In this they were unsuccessful, and the general who had defeated them became governor. This was in 1470 A.D. This new governor also promptly threw off his allegiance, and ruled as King for eleven years, in such fashion as to earn the nickname of the "Bilu," or ogre. His son succeeded, but was soon assassinated by a nephew, who seized the throne in 1485 A.D.

In spite of his very questionable mode of seizing the throne, this man seems to have been very much more capable than his predecessors. The King of Burma was persuaded to send him a white umbrella, and other ensigns of royalty, thereby acknowledging the independence of Taungu. The new King of Taungu also set up a claim to descent from the last King of Pagan. The authenticity of this claim is very doubtful, but it helped to attract to his kingdom Burmans who were becoming dissatisfied with the rule of the Shan Kings in Ava. One of them, who succeeded to the throne of Ava in 1520 A.D., thoroughly disgusted the Burmese by persecuting the Buddhist monks, and this gave a great additional impetus to the emigration to Taungu. The ruler there came to be looked on as the last hope of the Burmese race, and his claim to descent from the Kings of Pagan was not questioned. During his long reign of forty-five years he consolidated the power of Taungu. At his accession it was merely a small, though very troublesome and rebellious province of Ava. He at once got its independence acknowledged, and his alliance was sought by the Kings of Pegu and Siam, though border disputes led to occasional hostilities between Taungu and Pegu. He made a league with the King of Prome also against Ava, but nothing of much importance resulted from this league. It was he also who founded the city of Taungu, the rampart and ditch of which existed up to a recent period. He died in 1530 A.D., and was succeeded by his son, a boy of sixteen.

This lad, Tabeng Shwehti by name, took his position as representative of the ancient Kings of Burma very seriously, and determined, if possible, to win back what he conceived to be his heritage. He had the luck to have a kinsman, who was a capable general and thoroughly loyal to the young King. This general is best known as Bureng Naung, though that is a title, not a name. The first four years of Tabeng Shwehti's reign were spent in collecting arms, enrolling men, and in exciting the enthusiasm of the Burmese in Taungu by hopes of the restoration of the dominance of their race in its ancient seat. But it was judged better to commence by an attack on Pegu. The first attempts, however, were not successful. On the first occasion, the capital was so obstinately defended by two Shan officers that the besiegers were repulsed. The following year a further attempt was made, but the city was now defended by a contingent of Indian Mahomedans with firearms, and the besiegers had again to fall back. On the third attempt, a Portuguese galliot, commanded by Ferdinand de Morales, who had been sent from Goa to trade in Pegu, joined in the defence of the city. This is the first occasion on which Europeans took part in the wars of Burma. In spite of this Portuguese help to his enemy, Tabeng Shwehti succeeded in capturing Pegu on this occasion. The King of Pegu, the last of the dynasty established by Wareru, escaped to the delta, and died there. Tabeng Shwehti was now recognised as King of Pegu, and henceforward ruled from there; his hereditary kingdom, Taungu, being governed by the father of Bureng Naung.

To conciliate the people of Pegu, Talaings were appointed to govern the districts, while at the capital the defences were strengthened. The next thing was to subdue Martaban. Since the opening of trade with Europe by the Cape of Good Hope, Martaban had become a port of some consequence. In 1519 A.D. Antony Correa had concluded a treaty with the King of Pegu's Viceroy at Martaban, and had established a Portuguese depôt for produce at that port. After taking Pegu, Tabeng Shwehti summoned the Viceroy of Martaban to submit, but he, trusting to Portuguese help, refused to do so. Tabeng Shwehti and Bureng Naung accordingly set out, with a large army, to take Martaban. With seven European ships, heavily armed, in the port, and substantial earthworks on the land side, Bureng Naung could do little beyond establishing a strict blockade, in hopes of starving the town into surrender. The besiegers were repulsed in every attempt to force their way across the ditch and rampart, but they did succeed in setting fire to the ships, by means of blazing bamboo rafts set adrift when the tide would carry them to the ships. The siege went on for seven months, and then famine forced the town into surrender. Under a promise that his life would be spared, the Viceroy came out with his wife, children, and a numerous body of attendants, men and women. In spite of the promise, they were all put to an ignominious death. The conquerors secured immense booty; the city was set on fire and destroyed utterly. This was in 1540 A.D., and, after arranging for the government of Martaban, and establishing military posts near the frontiers of Zimmè and Siam, Tabeng Shwehti returned to Pegu, where he was consecrated King in accordance with the ancient ceremonies. He crowned the Pegu and Shwe Dagon pagodas with new *htis*, and while thus conciliating the Talaings by showing respect for their religious edifices, and by appointing Talaing officials, he continued to put forward prominently his claim to Burmese nationality and sovereignty.

As a first step towards breaking the Shan power in Ava, Tabeng Shwehti next attacked Prome. This town was strongly fortified, so the general, Bureng Naung, determined to starve it into surrender. The King at Ava, however, sent down an army to relieve his son-in-law, who was then King, or governor, of Prome. The King of Arakan also sent an army to repel the invader. Bureng Naung marched first to meet the Shan army from Ava, and utterly defeated it, the Portuguese gunners, whom he had brought with him, helping very materially in bringing about this victory. The Shans fled to the north, and the Arakanese force was then defeated and scattered. Prome continued to hold out for a time, but by June, 1542, hunger compelled the inhabitants to surrender. The King, Queen, and the chief officers were put to death, and a relative of Bureng Naung's was appointed governor, or tributary King, of Prome.

These conquests of Bureng Naung, and the claims of Tabeng Shwehti to Burmese nationality and sovereignty, raised the hopes of the Burmese race. The Shan King then reigning in Ava had made himself hated by both Shans and Burmese, on account of his cruelty, his persecution of the monks, and his sacrilegious plunder of pagodas. About the same time as the fall of Prome a successful conspiracy in Ava rid the country of this cruel and irreligious King. Shan influence, however, was still powerful enough to put another Shan on the throne.

The new King at once realised the danger of Tabeng Shwehti's possession of Prome, so his first act was to try and recover that town. Bureng Naung met this army promptly, defeated it, and chased the fugitives to the very gates of Ava, and on his way back occupied for a time the ancient capital, Pagan. This was in 1544 A.D., but the Shan power was still too strong to be successfully attacked in Ava, so Bureng Naung returned to Pegu. But, to keep prominently forward his claim to sovereignty over the whole country, Tabeng Shwehti was now solemnly consecrated as King of Kings, the tributary Kings of Prome, Taungu and Martaban doing homage to him as their over-lord. At the same time, Bureng Naung was formally appointed *Eingshemin*, or heir apparent.

Leaving Ava alone for the present, Tabeng Shwehti next turned his attention to Arakan. In 1546 he managed to take Sandoway, but the capital being too strongly fortified to be taken by assault, and news of a Siamese incursion on Tavoy having reached him, he had to leave Arakan alone for the present, and turn his attention to Siam. By the close of 1548 A.D. his army was assembled at Martaban, a body of Portuguese gunners under James Soarez, being part of it. This army penetrated as far as Ayuthia, which was then the capital of Siam, but could not take it, and there being considerable difficulty in feeding the army, Tabeng Shwehti had to accept the advice of Bureng Naung and order a retreat. The Siamese incessantly attacked the retreating invaders, thousands of whom were killed, or died of hunger and disease. Fortunately, the son-in-law of the Siamese King was taken prisoner in a skirmish, and, as the price of his release, the Burmo-Talaing army was allowed to retire without further molestation.

Tabeng Shwehti was still only thirty-six years of age, but after this unsuccessful invasion of Siam he gave himself up to debauchery, and became incapable of any proper attention to his duties. A nephew of James Soarez became his boon companion, and supplied him with liquor, until the king became a confirmed drunkard. Bureng Naung assumed the office of regent, banished the Portuguese youth who had led the King astray, and did what he could to carry on the work of restoring the empire. But the Talaings were chafing under the constant demands on them for military service, and Tabeng Shwehti's present condition excited their contempt. Under these circumstances, a rebellion, headed by a scion of the old royal house of Pegu, was successful, Tabeng Shwehti was treacherously killed, and Bureng Naung had to retire to Taungu. There his half-brother shut the gates against him, and, for a time, the enterprise which he and Tabeng Shwehti had taken up with such high hopes, and carried out with so much success in the beginning, seemed to have failed utterly. There appeared to be every chance of the country being again distracted by a number of small states always at war with each other.

Everything seemed to be lost, but Bureng Naung took up a position on the skirt of the mountains and waited his opportunity. In Pegu, two claimants were fighting for the throne, and in Upper Burma, also, the authority of the new King at Ava was becoming more and more restricted, new Kings springing up in various places. Bureng Naung's reputation attracted to him many people who desired to secure one fairly powerful kingdom instead of a number of warring kinglets. His adherents may have been chiefly Burmese, but there were, doubtless, Talaings also, and, possibly even some Shans. In a short time he was strong enough to take Taungu, and was crowned there as the successor of his father. He then marched across the hills and took Prome, after which all the country up the Irrawaddy, as far as Pagan, submitted to him. In 1551 A.D. he succeeded in taking Pegu also. There he was consecrated King of Kings, and his eldest son was declared heir-apparent. Two years later he commenced operations against Ava, but the fear of a powerful King being established there made the Shan chiefs curb their mutual jealousies, and co-operate against the common foe. This was in 1553 A.D. By the next year Bureng Naung had collected a great army and a considerable flotilla, with which, after the rainy season was over, he again advanced to attack Ava. On this occasion he had with him a bodyguard of four hundred Portuguese, dressed in uniform, and armed with arquebuses. In March, 1555, a general assault was made, and Ava fell to the conqueror. The Shan King was sent as a prisoner to Pegu. Bureng Naung returned there also after some months, and continued to regard Pegu as his capital. Though the Shan power in Ava was now effectually broken, the country to the north of it was still in the hands of independent Shan chiefs. In 1557 A.D., however, an opportunity occurred of interfering in one of their endless disputes, which Bureng Naung promptly seized. He was able to over-run the whole country as far as the Patkoi range, which separates Burma from Assam. The Shans were pursued into the mountains, and two powerful chiefs swore fealty to the King of Burma. Religious reforms were introduced, and the worship of the Shan people was brought into conformity with the Buddhism of Burma. The utterly heterodox custom which had prevailed among them of sacrificing an elephant, a horse, or even slaves, at the funeral of a chief, was strictly prohibited, and seems to have ceased from that time.

As this marks the end of the Shan dominion, which had been so fruitful of discord, by the constant uprising of petty kingdoms, it will be well to end this chapter here. Bureng Naung was now the monarch of all Burma, excepting Arakan, and the more remote Shan States. Their geographical position renders their inclusion of less importance. The important thing was to have brought the whole of the Irrawaddy, and sea-coasts of Pegu and Martaban, under one rule.

CHAPTER V.

A.D. 1558 TO 1599

BURENG NAUNG, the Branginoco of the Portuguese, had effectually broken the power of the Shans, and had he been content with this achievement, and devoted the remainder of his long reign to consolidating his kingdom, he would probably have founded a much stronger and more permanent kingdom than he actually did. But the Kings of Burma seem to have been particularly prone to the malady known as "swelled head." One or two conquests led them to push on further and further; they laid countries waste, and established tributary Kings, who took the first favourable opportunity of throwing off their allegiance. If those who had helped Bureng Naung to his supremacy thought the country was to have rest from war, as a result of establishing one powerful King instead of a number of small ones, they must have been bitterly disappointed. The country, as a whole, merely gained long and exhausting wars abroad instead of perpetual wars at home. Still, even that was some gain, as those who remained behind could, at least, cultivate the fields in peace.

In 1558, Bureng Naung marched to Zimmè, conquered that, and made the King a tributary. Then he went to Ava and received the homage of the Shan chiefs up to the frontier of China. They, however, were exempted from tribute, possibly because that might have given offence to China. Returning to Pegu, in May, 1559, he bent his energies to pagoda building, and to stopping the Mahomedans in Pegu from sacrificing animals. He went further, and more or less compelled a number of these foreigners to conform to Buddhism. This is very unusual, as the Buddhist kings of Burma have generally accorded complete religious liberty to foreigners resident in the country. This religious zeal gave the country three years' respite from war, but eventually led to an invasion of Siam. The King of that country was known to have four white elephants, and Bureng Naung was bent on getting at least one of them. No Buddhist King in Indo-China can be quite happy without a white elephant. An insignificant border dispute was made the pretext for invasion. An immense army of Burmese, Shans, and Talaings, marched into Siam, and invested Ayuthia. It was not, however, until March, 1564, that the city surrendered. The King of Siam is said to have consented to this surrender because he was disheartened by the capture of three Portuguese ships, which were moored near the shore and supported by batteries. It is remarkable how ubiquitous in Indo-China the Portuguese seem to have been by this time. The King of Siam, his queens, and his younger son, were carried away as captives to Pegu, the elder son being left to govern the country as a tributary King.

Bureng Naung then set out to punish the King of Zimmè for not having presented himself when the Burmese army passed through his country on the way to Ayuthia ; but, hearing that a rebellion had broken out in Pegu, he hastened back there, leaving his son to punish the King of Zimmè. On reaching Pegu he found that many fine buildings he had erected had been burnt by the rebels. He seems to have had no difficulty in crushing that rebellion, and immediately set to work to build a still more magnificent palace, but had to go to help his son, who evidently lacked his father's genius for war, and was not progressing satisfactorily in Zimmè. During his advance another rebellion, headed by a Shan captive, broke out in Pegu. Thousands of Talaings joined in it ; and the officers in command at Pegu became panic-stricken. The captive King of Ava, however, pointed out that the rebels were merely an unarmed rabble, so he was given a force to go out and defeat them, which he did. Bureng Naung had hurried back on hearing of this rebellion, and was so enraged at finding that many of his fine buildings outside the city walls had been burnt, that he pursued the rebels and captured thousands of them. These, along with their families, he proposed to enclose in a bamboo building and burn the whole lot. But the Buddhist monks protested against this wholesale slaughter, so he pardoned all except the leaders. It would be interesting to know how he showed his gratitude to the captive King of Ava, whom he had deposed in 1554, and who acted loyally to him on this occasion, attacking the rebels, and defeating them, when Bureng Naung's own officers were panic-stricken ; but this we are not told.

Shortly after Bureng Naung's return to Pegu, his son returned from Zimmè, having successfully concluded his operations there. He brought with him a number of captives. After this there was another short respite from war, but by the end of 1568 another invasion of Siam became necessary. As long as his father, brother and other relatives were captives in Pegu, they were practically hostages for the good behaviour of the tributary King of Siam, and while they were there he made no effort to regain his independence. But the brother died, the father became a monk and obtained permission to

COLOSSAL IMAGE AT PEGU

Photograph by Mr P. Klier, Rangoon

go to his own country to worship. The son's widow was also allowed to return with her children. This leniency on Bureng Naung's part was ill-judged, as, immediately his relatives were out of Burma, the tributary King of Siam asserted his independence. In this he was backed by his father, who promptly became a layman again. This led to a fresh invasion by Bureng Naung, but the Siamese made a desperate defence, and the Burmese army suffered great loss. When things were nearly desperate, Bureng Naung resorted to stratagem. One of his Siamese adherents pretended to desert, and entered Ayuthia with irons on his legs. The King there received him gladly, and appointed him to a high command. This trust he betrayed by secretly opening the gates one night to the Burmese army. The siege of seven months had failed to reduce the city, but when the besiegers had obtained an entry by this trick they soon put down all opposition, and the city was given up to plunder. This was in August, 1569. In the history of Siam it is assigned to 1555, but that is manifestly wrong. The Venetian traveller, Cæsar Fredericke, was in Pegu at this time, and he dates the King's return in 1569. In the Burmese history the return is dated 1570, the King having undertaken some minor expeditions against the King of Laos, and other minor potentates, on the return journey. The army that went out is said to have numbered two hundred thousand men, but only a small remnant returned.

After the return to Pegu there were, of course, costly offerings to the pagodas, and a new ambition took hold of the King. He wanted a share of foreign trade, so he built a ship of his own and sent it to Ceylon and to the ports of Southern India. He seems to have been imbued with indomitable energy, which he was ready to throw into the work in hand, whether that was war, religious reform, building, trade, or the administration of justice. His only rest seems to have been change of occupation. Cæsar Fredericke describes how "the King sitteth every day, in person, to hear the suits of his subjects, up aloft in a great hall, on a tribunal seat, with his barons round about," while the petitioners are on the ground, forty paces distant, with their supplications in their hands. "If the King think it good to do them that favour or justice they demand, then he commandeth to take the presents out of their hands; but if he think their demand be not just, or according to right, he commandeth them away without taking their gifts or presents." It was a very primitive method of administering justice, but Cæsar Fredericke seems to have been greatly impressed, both by the power of Bureng Naung and by his justice. Regarding the power he says:—"the King of Pegu hath not any army or power by sea, but, in the land, for people, dominions, gold and silver, he far exceeds the power of the Great Turk in treasure and strength." As to his justice, more especially towards foreigners, the following is very high praise, for an Eastern autocrat in the sixteenth century: "If any Christian dieth in the kingdom of Pegu, the King and his officers rest heirs of a third of his goods, and there hath never been any deceit or fraud used in this matter. I have known many rich men that have dwelled in Pegu, and in their age have desired to go into their own country to die there, and have departed with all their goods and substance, without let or trouble."

We need not follow the military expeditions of the next few years, which were merely punitive ones against revolting chiefs both in Laos and among the northern Shans. It was on his return, at the end of 1576, from a successful expedition against the latter, that Bureng Naung received the welcome intelligence that a ship had arrived from Ceylon, bringing the holy tooth of Guadama Buddha. The conquest of Siam had, of course, provided him with white elephants, but his efforts to get a sacred tooth had, so far, proved unavailing. The real tooth, or what was universally accepted as such, had been taken at Jaffna, in 1560, and had been destroyed by Don Constantine, the Viceroy of India, though Bureng Naung had then offered a sum equal to over forty thousand pounds sterling to ransom it. With the real tooth destroyed, however, two other "real teeth" promptly sprang up. One of these was in the possession of the King of Colombo, with whom Bureng Naung had been negotiating for some time for the sacred relic. Two years before, a Singhalese princess had arrived in Pegu, and been received with high honour, though, according to a Portuguese historian, the lady was only the daughter of a chamberlain. Now the tooth had arrived along with a letter from the King of Colombo, saying that he was the only orthodox King in Ceylon. Seeing that he had been baptised as a Christian, his Buddhist orthodoxy is open to question. His kingdom, too, was very restricted, his authority being confined to Colombo. Altogether he seems to have been a shifty character, quite capable of palming off a chamberlain's daughter as a princess. Whether Bureng Naung believed the tooth to be genuine or not, it was good policy to receive it as such, so a deputation of high officials was sent to receive it in a costly golden vase. In addition to this his reward to the King of Colombo was so munificent that the King of Kandy, on hearing of it, offered Bureng Naung a true daughter and a true tooth. This offer does not seem to have been accepted, if it was ever really made.

The story rests on the authority of a Portuguese historian, but seems probable enough. Bureng Naung had no fleet, so any King in Ceylon was well out of his reach, and could run risks of incurring his wrath which those accessible by land would scarcely venture on. The King of Kandy's offer would scarcely be preserved in Burmese chronicles, as it tended to throw discredit on the tooth in hand, to say nothing of the Singhalese "princess." Moreover it does not do to have too many relics, as that tends to their being lightly esteemed.

It is somewhat remarkable that during all this time nothing should have been done to bring Arakan into subjection. But Bureng Naung's hands were sufficiently full of work elsewhere, and there were various reasons for hesitating in the matter of Arakan. A fleet was not an actual necessity, no doubt, as troops had often invaded Arakan by land before, but a fleet would certainly facilitate the invasion. Moreover, Arakan's relations with Bengal were now different from what they had been, and so astute a man as Bureng Naung may well have hesitated before the risk of becoming embroiled in Indian politics. He seems never to have forgotten, however, that Arakan rightly belongs to Burma, and towards the close of his life he determined to try to conquer it. Burmese history says that he had sent ambassadors to the Emperor Akbar, whose general had conquered Bengal in 1576. These ambassadors did not go further probably than the governor of Bengal, and their mission may have been merely to ascertain whether the occupation of Arakan would be regarded as an act of hostility by the great Emperor Akbar. Bureng Naung was supreme in his own field, but he was not a rash fool, and knew well enough, probably, that he was no match for Akbar.

Be this as it may, the invasion was begun in 1580. A large fleet of vessels, mere boats probably, was collected, and some eighty thousand men, including the crews, set out by sea. Near Cape Negrais, however, the fleet met some Portuguese ships, and a somewhat curious sea-fight seems to have taken place. The Portuguese took some of the Burmese, or Talaing, fleet, but had to withdraw on account of the number of the latter. The Portuguese estimated the number at thirteen hundred sail. The remainder of Bureng Naung's fleet made their way to the southern coast of Arakan, where they landed and marched to Sandoway. Here, however, they remained inactive for twelve months. Bureng Naung was not with them himself, or the result might have been different. He sent on reinforcements, but in November, 1581, Bureng Naung died, and with his death the invasion of Arakan collapsed. He had reigned for thirty years, and for a long time before that he had been the general of Tabeng Shwehti. First as general and then as King he had been for between forty and fifty years the great force in Indo-China. If ever there was a strenuous life it was his ; and, like Anawrata, five centuries earlier, his personality stands out as that of a capable, and on the whole, a just man, who did his work manfully, according to such lights as he had. Such characters are uncommon enough among autocrats anywhere, but even Oriental history is not so wholly lacking in them as many people suppose.

Bureng Naung was succeeded by his eldest son, called in the Talaing chronicle Nanda Bureng, and in the Burmese chronicle Gna-su-Daraga. It will be more convenient to adhere to the Talaing name. Nanda Bureng had already shown, in the Zimmè campaign, that he lacked his father's military skill. He was now to prove that he equally lacked his administrative ability.

He succeeded to the throne without dispute, and at once recalled the army from Arakan. The Kings of Prome and Taungu came to Pegu and did homage, as also did the King of Siam. But the King of Ava made excuses, and tried to draw Prome and Taungu into a conspiracy to shake off the supremacy of Pegu. Nanda Bureng discovered this, and, suspecting that many of his own officers were in the plot, he caused them, their wives and children, to be burnt to death. This atrocious punishment was witnessed by Gasparo Balbi, a jeweller of Venice, who happened to be in Pegu at the time. He puts the number executed at four thousand, which may be an exaggeration, but, though a traveller in the sixteenth century must have seen many an injustice, this holocaust evidently struck him as particularly revolting. He mentions his "great compassion and grief that little children, without any fault, should suffer such martyrdom."

Nanda Bureng then marched on Ava, along with the Kings of Prome and Taungu. They defeated the King of Ava, who fled and escaped across the Chinese frontier. Another tributary King was put in his place. The King of Siam had been summoned to assist in the war against Ava, but instead of doing so, he hovered about Pegu, intending, apparently, to attack it, should Nanda Bureng meet with a reverse in Upper Burma. On hearing of the defeat of the King of Ava, however, he retired to Martaban, seized a number of the inhabitants there, and carried them off to Siam. To avenge this insult, an expedition was sent off in hot haste, but it was forced to retreat with heavy loss. Nanda Bureng then set off at the head of his army to punish the King of Siam, but his lack of administrative qualities was shown in the defective arrangements made. Thousands died from want and exposure, and a disastrous retreat was made, the King reaching Pegu with only a small escort. Two more equally unsuccessful expeditions were made into Siam under Nanda Bureng's son, who was killed in the second of these, in February, 1593. After this, Nanda Bureng seems to have abandoned himself to blind fury. He trusted no one, put his most loyal officers to death, and even killed many Talaing monks. Thousands of people abandoned their country and fled. The rich delta districts became depopulated from war, famine and migration. The King of Siam invaded the country, and when he retired a number of Talaings went with him. He seems to have annexed Martaban and Tavoy, and to have set up his own tributary Kings in these places. The King of Arakan sent a fleet and seized Syriam, which was then the chief seaport of the delta. The King of Taungu, co-operating with the Arakanese fleet, took Pegu, seized Nanda Bureng, and sent him as a prisoner to Taungu, where, soon after, he was put to death. The King of Taungu carried away a great part of the plunder, while the prince of Arakan received a portion of the treasure, a white elephant, and a princess, as his share. He also retained possession of Syriam, where he left a garrison.

This general break-up of the empire founded by Bureng Naung occurred in 1599. In eighteen years his son had managed to lose everything; the country—all of it, at least, that had not been annexed by Siam—was again split up among a lot of petty kinglets, all claiming independence, and ready to fight with each other on every occasion. As Sir Arthur Phayre says:—" Thus the great empire of united Pegu and Burma, which a generation before had excited the wonder of European travellers, was utterly broken up; and the wide delta of the Irrawaddy, with a soil fertile as Egypt, and in a geographical position commanding the outlet of a great natural highway, was abandoned by those who might claim to represent the ancient rulers, and left to be parcelled out by petty local chiefs and European adventurers." The collapse was even more sudden than Sir Arthur Phayre represents. Ralph Fitch, an English merchant, was in Pegu in 1586 or 1587, and he describes the country as being still in a prosperous state then. He was impressed by the magnificence of the capital, and describes the streets as "the fairest that ever I saw." He says of the King, that he keeps great state, but "at my being there he went to Odia (Ayuthia) with three hundred thousand men and five thousand elephants." The final collapse was in 1599, only twelve or thirteen years after Ralph Fitch's visit to Pegu.

CHAPTER VI.

A.D. 1600 TO 1752

SOMETHING very like chaos succeeded the death of Nanda Bureng. Not only did various indigenous kinglets set up as independent Kings, but the Portuguese added greatly to the general confusion. Portuguese ships swarmed about the coast, more especially along the coast of Arakan. Many of them were little better than pirates, but they had to be taken into account. After the taking of Syriam, which was then the port of Pegu, the King of Arakan was astute enough to see that there was little chance of his being able to hold it, without the concurrence of the Portuguese. He had in his palace a young Portuguese, who had originally been a ship-boy, and had afterwards served as a menial in the palace. To conciliate the Portuguese generally, this young man, Philip de Brito, was sent to Syriam to take charge of the custom-house there, and to represent the King with his own countrymen. The Arakanese governor of Syriam had no authority over the Portuguese there, who were guaranteed the enjoyment of their own laws. It was a fatuous arrangement, and de Brito was not slow to see his chances and to avail himself of them. He got permission to build a custom-house of brick, and then he built a fort as a necessary protection to the custom-house. His next step was to induce a Portuguese officer, Salvador Ribeyro, to expel the Arakanese governor. This done, de Brito seized the governorship himself. He then appointed Ribeyro governor while he himself went off to Goa to interview the Viceroy and to offer to hold Syriam for him.

Meantime, the expelled governor had obtained from the King of Arakan a force to enable him to retake Syriam. The King of Prome added a contingent to this force, and, on their way through the Talaing country, a number of Talaings joined them. This mixed force came down the Irrawaddy, invested Syriam, and continued the siege for eight months. De Brito was still away, but Ribeyro made a determined defence. To prevent his countrymen from being driven by hunger to escape, he burned the three ships he had in port. At length relief sent by the Portuguese Viceroy arrived, and the besieging force retired. Ribeyro's next care was to conciliate the Talaings, and, so successfully did he do this that when de Brito returned, with the title of captain-general, and with the Viceroy's niece as his bride, the Talaings were ready to accept him as King of Pegu. He had six ships with him ; he accepted the crown in the name of the King of Portugal ; he put the fortifications in order, and built a church. Syriam had been taken by the Arakanese in 1596, but de Brito did not go to Syriam till 1600, as one of the Jesuit Fathers mentions in a letter that he travelled from Arakan to Pegu with de Brito in that year. His return from Goa must have been in 1602 or 1603, so it had only taken three years, at most, for him to rise from the position of a menial in the palace to kingship. In those days of general confusion throughout Burma, the rapid rise to a throne is not so very remarkable, perhaps, but that the proud Viceroy of India should have allowed his niece to marry an adventurer of the kind is extraordinary.

Now that de Brito had the support of the Viceroy, the King of Arakan hesitated to attack him, but, eventually, in conjunction with the King of Taungu, a flotilla was sent. The result, however, was disastrous; the Portuguese ships attacked the flotilla, and the Prince of Arakan was taken prisoner. De Brito had the sense and good feeling to treat with respect this Prince, Min Khamaung, the one who had originally taken Syriam; but he demanded fifty thousand crowns for his release. This the King of Arakan refused to pay, but when a second attempt to take the town had failed, he paid the ransom, and the young Prince was set free. This was in 1604. De Brito was now secure, and with any prudence might have made his kingdom a great province under the crown of Portugal. The Talaings sought his friendship; the King of Taungu entered into alliance with him; and his son married a daughter of the King of Martaban. But his rapid rise seems to have turned his head, and, instead of conciliating the people, he outraged their religious ideas by plundering the pagodas and by compelling the people to become Christians.

While he was thus preparing a rod for his own back, a younger son of Bureng Naung had managed to secure Ava, with a portion of Upper Burma, and had gradually recovered some authority over the neighbouring Shan States. He did not live long enough, however, to do more than this, as he died in 1605. On his deathbed he charged his son, Maha Dhamma Raja, to re-establish the empire of Bureng Naung. The first years of his reign were spent in reducing the Shan States to subjection, then he took Prome, after an investment of eight months. This was in 1608. Two years later he marched against Taungu, and forced the King there to become his tributary, and to give some members of his family as hostages for his fidelity. De Brito, however, resented this as a breach of the alliance with himself, so in 1612, he marched to Taungu, plundered the city, burned the palace, and carried off the unhappy King as a prisoner. By the end of the same year, the Burmese King had gathered a considerable force round Syriam. He had no guns to batter the fort, but he established a strict blockade to starve the town into surrender. He was also determined that de Brito should not escape.

Although de Brito had been so recklessly aggressive, he had neglected the most obvious precautions. He was short of powder, and he had only one hundred Portuguese in the garrison, the remainder having been allowed to go to India. After about a month he was compelled by hunger to beg for mercy. To this no answer was returned. At this juncture a fleet of fifty Arakanese boats appeared, to try and regain Syriam for Arakan, but the investing Burmese force managed to overcome the Arakanese, and secure the boats. At length a Talaing in the town opened one of the gates at night, the Burmese entered and soon overcame the famished garrison. This was in April, 1613. De Brito was impaled on a high stake before his own house, and suffered agony for three days till death released him. His son, who was at Martaban, was also secured and put to death. All the leading Portuguese were executed, while the remainder were sent as slaves to Ava. De Brito's wife was also sent as a slave to Ava. It was a humiliating position for a niece of the Portuguese Viceroy, and a very heavy penalty for some ten years of having been a queen. The whole episode of de Brito's rapid rise and equally rapid fall is eminently characteristic of the time. A few days after the fall of Syriam five ships arrived from Goa, laden with powder and arms sent by the Viceroy. Somewhat later a ship belonging to de Brito's wife came in from Achin, laden with provisions. All but one of these were taken by the Burmese; the King of Martaban submitted, and became a tributary; a Siamese force came to watch events, but did not interfere; so Maha Dhamma Raja had done a good deal towards recovering the empire his grandfather had won and his uncle had lost.

The next few years were spent in reducing to subjection various outlying parts of the Empire. Tavoy and Tenasserim were wrested from the Siamese, though the latter place was defended by Portuguese in the service of the King of Siam. By 1617 the King had got things into order, Burmese, Shans and Talaings being appointed to administer the districts. Burma proper, Prome, Taungu and Zimmè were governed by tributary Kings; Martaban and Tenasserim by governors; and Pegu was under the direct government of Maha Dhamma Raja himself. He entered into communication with the Viceroy at Goa, with the Emperor Jahangir in India, and with the Sultan of Achin. In the last case, at least, some joint action against the Portuguese was contemplated. These people swarmed all along the coast, and were hated on account of their attacks on native vessels at sea. They were practically pirates, and varied the proceedings by landing and plundering villages. The Arakanese coast was their chief haunt, but they were a source of terror all along the coasts of both Burma and India.

The following incidents will show what a scourge the Portuguese were. Among other settlements they had was one called Dianga, about twenty miles south of Chittagong. The settlers did a thriving trade with Bengal, combining this more or less honest trade with piracy. After de Brito's treachery at Syriam, the King of Arakan attacked Dianga and took it, slaughtering most of the inhabitants. A few escaped, among them one Sebastian Gonzales, an adventurer of the de Brito type. He had come from Europe and enlisted as a soldier. Then he became owner of a small vessel, with which he traded on the coast of Bengal. He was in Dianga with a cargo of salt when the Arakanese attacked that settlement. After his escape from there, he lived for some time by plundering the villages on the Arakanese coast. He was then employed by a small potentate, the Raja of Bakla, in what is now the district of Bakirgunj, to fight another small quasi-independent potentate in the island of Sundeep. For this enterprise Gonzales managed to secure a flotilla of forty sail, manned by four hundred Portuguese sailors. With this force he attacked and took the port of Sundeep, putting the whole of the inhabitants to death. Then he threw over the Raja of Bakla and appropriated to his own use, not only Sundeep, but two neighbouring islands as well. About this time the governor of Chittagong, having offended his brother, the King of Arakan, fled to Sundeep. Gonzales received him and married his sister ; but the governor died suddenly, was poisoned, it was said, and Gonzales seized all his treasure.

The King of Arakan had every reason to distrust the Portuguese, but as the governor of Bengal was determined to recover the country east of the Megna, which had submitted to the King of Arakan, the latter entered into a league with Gonzales. The King of Arakan marched from Chittagong with his army, and was successful in his first encounters with the Moghul troops. Meanwhile at sea, Gonzales had considered his own interests only, and set to work in his own treacherous way. He called the Arakanese captains to a consultation and murdered them. After that the vessels fell an easy prey, and

Gonzales added the Arakanese fleet to his own. The King of Arakan soon found that he could not stand against further Moghul reinforcements sent against him, so he retreated to Chittagong, and, leaving a strong garrison there, returned to his own capital. There he impaled a nephew of Gonzales, who had been given to him, apparently, as a hostage.

Gonzales was, evidently, one of those who think that everyone else should act honourably to him, however dishonourably he might act himself. He resented the execution of his nephew, so he entered the Arakan river with several ships, plundered the villages, and captured some European merchant vessels—probably Dutch which were lying there. At this juncture the King of Arakan died, in 1612, and was succeeded by his son, Min Khamaung, who had taken Syriam some years before. The young King determined to attack Gonzales in his stronghold, so he marched to Chittagong, his fleet keeping near the coast, in touch with the army. But he came into collision with the forces of the Raja of Tipperah, and had to retire without attaining his object. Gonzales sent messengers to the Viceroy at Goa, urging that all he had done was to avenge the murder of the Portuguese at Dianga, and offering, if supported, to pay a yearly tribute to Portugal. As a further inducement, he suggested that the conquest of Arakan would be easy and would yield a rich reward. The Viceroy fell in with this suggestion, and sent a fleet of fourteen galliots, under Don Francis de Menesis, which reached the mouth of the Arakan river towards the close of 1615. Without waiting for the arrival of Gonzales, Don Francis went up the river, but was driven back by the Arakanese and some Dutch vessels which happened to be there. A few days later Gonzales arrived with fifty sail, mostly small craft, so a fresh attempt was made. At first this promised to be successful, partly through the reckless courage of Gonzales, but when Don Francis was killed, and the galliot of Gaspar de Abreu was taken, the Portuguese fleet retired and set sail for Goa. Nothing was left for Gonzales but to get back to Sundeep, which he did. Two years later Min Khamaung attacked him there, put most of the inhabitants to death, and destroyed the fortifications. Gonzales escaped, but what became of him is not known. The Portuguese historian dismisses him with the remark that " his pride was humbled and his villanies punished." His murder of the Arakanese captains was certainly as foul a crime as could well be committed, and his numerous treacheries deserved severe punishment ; yet he escaped the agonising torture of impalement, which his treachery had brought on his nephew, and which de Brito, a less unprincipled scoundrel, had endured.

The history of Arakan for the better part of a century after this, is more intimately connected with that of India than with that of Burma. Min Khamaung pushed his conquests in India as far as Dacca. His successor enforced the payment of tribute from Dacca, and varied the proceedings by a marauding expedition into Pegu. In the time of his successor, a refugee Mahomedan prince sought an asylum in Arakan, arriving at the capital in 1660 A.D. At first he was well received, but a large sum being offered for him by Aurungzebe's general, the King's disposition towards him changed. The refugee, in self-defence, headed a Mahomedan insurrection, but, failing in this, fled to the hills, was taken prisoner and put to death. His bodyguard of archers was taken into the service of the King of Arakan. This, in the end, proved a disastrous mistake, as, later on, this foreign corps became notorious for turbulence and violence, practically disposing of the throne at their own caprice. Dacca had been lost before this, but the Arakanese, in conjunction with the Portuguese and other European adventurers,made incursions into Bengal, plundering the country up to the gates of Dacca. The governor of Bengal, however, managed to detach the Europeans from the service of Arakan, by giving them land south of Dacca, still known as Feringibazaar. This done, he was able to deal with the Arakanese, and in 1666, he drove them out of Chittagong; about two thousand prisoners were secured and sold as slaves. The Arakanese had held Chittagong for over a century, but after its loss, they never gained any permanent footing beyond Arakan, though plundering expeditions still crossed the border from time to time. Towards the close of the seventeenth century, the archers of the bodyguard practically took all power into their own hands, setting up and deposing Kings at will. Early in the eighteenth century, an Arakanese of determined character, though not of royal blood, overcame the guards and seized the throne. He made incursions both into Bengal and into the Irrawaddy valley, but they were mere marauding incursions, ending in no permanent conquest. He had several successors on the throne, among whom were several usurpers, but Arakan never regained her former power.

We must now return to Upper Burma and Pegu, where Maha Dhamma Raja had managed to get back a very considerable part of the empire his grandfather, Bureng Naung, had ruled. He and his successors, up to the middle of the seventeenth century, kept the empire together, ruling at first from Pegu, but in 1634 A.D. the King then reigning made Ava the capital. In 1659,

Chinese invaders appeared, and plundered the country up to the gates of Ava. They attacked the city, but were repulsed, mainly by the native Christians, descendants of the Portuguese captives, who served the guns on the walls. The Chinese retired for a time, but came back a few months later. On that occasion they seem to have been driven away by the difficulty of getting supplies. This shortage of supplies was felt by the Burmese also, as the plundering of these marauding bands had interfered with agriculture. The people of Ava accused the King of indifference to their sufferings, and of allowing the inmates of the palace to profit by the sale of rice stored therein. This led to a successful insurrection, headed by the King's brother, who secured the throne. He drove the Chinese out of the country, but in 1662 there were further troubles with the Chinese. From this time onwards, the power of the Kings at Ava declines. Zimmè was taken by the Siamese, and afterwards recovered by the Burmese. The chief of Manipur occupied the Kubo valley without opposition. Other outlying districts were lost ; a Burmese army was defeated on the frontier of Manipur, some time after the occupation of the Kubo valley by the Manipuris, and Zimmè was again lost.

Worse than all these losses of outlying portions of the empire, was the growing disaffection among the Talaings. They bitterly resented the transfer of the capital from Pegu to Ava, and the governors sent from Ava oppressed the people. Nothing, not even the women's looms, escaped taxation. In 1740 A.D., the Burmese governor, Maung Tha Aung, set up as King of Pegu, under the impression that the King of Ava was not strong enough to call him to account. He reckoned, however, without the Talaings, who hated him, and promptly killed him. Then the King of Ava sent his uncle as governor, but the Talaings would have nothing to do with him, and murdered all his followers. At this time, the end of 1740, an insurrection broke out among a Shan colony to the north of Pegu. These Shans had been brought from their own country and settled there by Bureng Naung, nearly two centuries before this. They are called by the Burmese, Gwe Shans. The insurrection of 1740 was headed by a man said in the Talaing history to be a Gwe Shan, though he claimed to be an offshoot of the royal house reigning at Ava. Such claims to royal blood, however, need never be taken very seriously in Burmese history. What is much more important is that he had been brought up away from the enervating influence of palaces, among the Karens and Gwe Shans. He had also made himself popular among the Talaings, whose language he spoke. When the insurrection broke out he was living quietly as a monk in a monastery in Pegu, but he threw off the monk's robe and was soon proclaimed King of Pegu, under the title of Mengtara Buddha Kethi.

The next six years were spent in various expeditions against the Burmese, but without much tangible result. The Talaings succeeded in taking Prome and Taungu, and even ravaged the country almost up to the gates of Ava. In the third of these advances, however, the Talaings were badly beaten, and had to retreat to Prome. Mengtara Buddha Kethi was an astrologer, and casting his own horoscope, he became convinced that his only course was to abdicate, so that the Talaing people should not be involved in the disasters portended for himself. The Talaings begged him to remain, but he refused. He wandered through Laos and Cochin-China, and entered China. After some years he returned and settled in Zimmè.

The whole of this episode of Mengtara Buddha Kethi and his successor is singularly different from the general course of Burmese history. Other monks have become laymen and secured a throne, but the subsequent abdication, from a purely altruistic motive, is unique. The selection of his successor is equally remarkable. A scribe in the palace managed to play the part of King for a few days, but he seems never to have been taken seriously by the people, and his kingship was never anything more than a farce, though it cost him his life. Among the chief adherents of Mengtara Buddha Kethi was one bearing the title of Binya Dala, who was said to be pre-eminent in ability. His colleagues seem to have been unanimous in electing him to the vacant throne. Doubtless they knew that if the Talaing country was to remain independent of Ava, the very best man that could be found was needed. But, even so, it is an unusual instance of altruism that personal ambitions should have been sunk so completely as to result in a genuine attempt to put the best man on the throne. He was probably a Shan, but that is uncertain. According to Burmese history, he had originally come from Zimmè to Pegu with elephants, was made master of the elephants by Mengtara Buddha Kethi, and gradually acquired influence. The Talaing chronicle says nothing of his origin, but manages to connect him with an old prophecy about native rulers. How he, a Shan from Zimmè, could be fitted in with such a prophecy is rather curious, but prophecies are sometimes wonderfully twisted when that will serve a purpose. To royal blood he seems to have made no claim, and that, also, was a new departure.

Binya Dala having been elected to the throne in a novel way, proceeded to do an unusual thing in taking the people into his confidence. After the ceremony of his consecration, he made a speech to the assembled court. He spoke of the former greatness of Pegu and announced his intention of bringing the King of Ava, and the other reigning Kings of the country into subjection, and of establishing again the empire of Bureng Naung in all its magnificence. For this purpose an army must be raised, the commander-in-chief of which would be Talaban. This is the first mention of a name afterwards famous in Pegu. Until this army was raised and a flotilla got ready to attack Ava in force, Binya Dala wisely refrained from any decisive action. But, from the frontier towns of Prome and Taungu, mixed bodies of Talaings and Gwe Shans made incursions into Upper Burma, penetrating at one time even beyond Ava. In 1750, the King of Burma sent an appeal to China for help against the Talaings. In reply to this appeal two Chinese or Manchu officers arrived with a hundred horsemen and a thousand foot-soldiers. In conjunction with the Burmese they attacked a Talaing stockade at Madara, but failed to take it, after which the Chinese contingent went back to China, leaving the Burmese and Talaings to fight out their quarrel by themselves.

By the time that the rains of 1751 were nearly over, Binya Dala found himself in a position to begin serious operations. He had collected an army of sixty thousand men and a large flotilla of boats, laden with supplies, and war boats to guard them. He had also secured fire-arms from European traders, and had in his service some Dutch mercenaries as well as the native Portuguese. By the beginning of 1752, Ava was invested by the invaders, who had met with no serious opposition on the way. In Ava, the King, the court and the people were in despair. No adequate preparations for defence had been made, and food soon became scarce. The soldiers deserted whenever a chance offered. Towards the end of March, the besiegers entered the outer city, and set it on fire. The inner city was defended by a high wall, but the defence was of the poorest description, the soldiers being weakened by hunger, and lacking any efficient leader. In two days the besiegers forced the gates and the foremost to enter made straight for the palace. The King was found in a large hall surrounded by his queens. They were at once secured, but well treated, and sent as captives to Pegu. The city of Ava was burned to the ground, and Binya Dala's brother, who had nominally commanded the invading army, returned to Pegu, taking with him the greater part of the army, while Talaban, who had been the real leader, was left in command at Ava to establish the rule of the Talaing King in Upper Burma. The Burmese had been so utterly crushed that no further resistance was expected from them. It was a natural enough conclusion under the circumstances, but nothing is so uncertain as the unforeseen, and it is always a mistake to be too confident.

CHAPTER VII.

A.D. 1752 TO 1760

THE crushing defeat which the Burmese had sustained seemed to assure the predominance of the Talaings and the revival of the empire of Bureng Naung. The Burmese King had been taken away captive to Pegu; his government had utterly broken down, and even before the fall of Ava, proclamations had been issued by the Talaing leaders summoning the administrative officers throughout the country to submit, and swear allegiance to the King of Pegu. One comparatively obscure official, however, refused to do so. This man's name was Aungzeya, which means Victor. This name is said to have been given him by his parents as a good omen. If it really had been given to him in childhood, it is, perhaps, the only instance in history of such a name being fully justified by after events. His first occupation seems to have been that of a hunter, which is looked down on by the Burmese, as it involves the taking of life. As the leader of a band of huntsmen, he came to be known as *Mutsobo*, the hunter captain, and his village as *Mutsobomyo*, the town of the hunter captain. It is now known as Shwebo. With a weak government at Ava, such a band of hunters would probably combine an occasional dacoity with their hunting, but of this there is no record, and possibly the band confined their operations to hunting. At the time of the Talaing invasion Aungzeya was the *Myo-thugyi*, and as such, responsible for the revenue collections of his district, and for the maintenance of order in it. From the first he declared he would not submit to the invaders, and when his parents begged him to submit, he replied that he could not swear allegiance to a Talaing King.

After the fall of Ava, the Talaing officer sent to collect the revenue from the country in which Mutsobomyo lay, deputed a subordinate with fifty men to that particular part. This party came to a village near Mutsobomyo and sent to summon Aungzeya as the *Myo-thugyi*. He came, but with forty men, surprised the fifty Talaings and killed them all. He fortified his village, and when a larger body of men came against him, he went out to meet them, and defeated them with great loss. After defeating a third force sent against him, he gave orders to his men to spare any Burmese and Shans who fought under the Talaing usurper. It was good policy to presume that they only did so under compulsion, and in this way he made his own resistance appear a national one. It is probable that it was at this time that he took the name Aungzeya, and that the story of his parents having given it to him in childhood was a later fabrication, along with claims to royal descent and wonderful portents at his birth. Talaban, who was in charge at Ava, saw the necessity for crushing this opposition, so he set off in person to reduce the stronghold at Mutsobomyo, but he failed in this and was recalled to Pegu. His successor was equally unsuccessful, and while the Talaing power declined in Upper Burma, that of Aungzeya increased. In Pegu the importance of Aungzeya's resistance seems not to have been realised, as no reinforcements were sent to the general in command at Ava. This was a fatal mistake, as every success brought fresh men to Aungzeya's standard. He had now proclaimed himself King, under the title of Alaungpaya, "embryo Buddha," a name which Europeans have corrupted into Alompra. He built a palace, and proclaimed that Mutsobomyo was to be the capital of Burma, under the name of Ratanathinga, which means the City of the Precious Priesthood. He seems to have had unlimited confidence in himself at all times, and his ambition was boundless.

It was not, however, until November, 1753, that Alompra found himself strong enough to attack Ava. Then he sent an army under one of his sons to encompass the city, and both banks of the river were held by a flotilla of boats, most of which had been captured from the Talaings. The Talaing general, having received no reinforcements from Pegu, and knowing that he could not count on the fidelity of the Burmese in Ava, came to the conclusion that discretion was the better part of valour, so he abandoned the city by night and got away with but little loss. Alompra's son at once entered, and took possession of the city in his father's name. Alompra himself came down and stayed three months in Ava, and then went up the river to make sure of the allegiance of the Shan chiefs. About this time Prome fell into the hands of the Burmese. Early in 1754, the Talaing King collected a large army and sent it away to retake Ava. The supreme command was placed in the hands of the King's brother, though his previous record scarcely afforded good grounds for confidence in his ability. Talaban was given the second command. The Talaings did not stop to retake Prome, but left a detachment to blockade it. Further on they met a Burmese army under the command of two of Alompra's sons. In this encounter the Burmese were defeated, and the Talaings continued their march to Ava, which they invested, their flotilla of boats giving them the command of the river. So far, all had gone well with them, but Alompra, issuing from Mutsobomyo, defeated a Talaing party which had been sent up the river to reconnoitre. Pursuing them, he encountered Talaban and forced him to retreat. The Talaing King's brother made no effort to help Talaban, and when the Burmese made a sally from Ava he made a hasty retreat to Prome, and on arriving there left Talaban to rally the army and remain before the town, while he himself fled to Pegu.

The Burmese were now in undisputed possession of Ava, but the Burmese garrison in Prome was sorely pressed, and made urgent appeals for relief. By this time the Talaing King was awakened to the importance of Prome, so a fresh army was sent to take it, towards the end of 1754. Before this army marched a fatal mistake was made in putting to death, on a charge of conspiracy, the captive King of Ava. This exasperated the Burmese, and, as Alompra said on hearing of it, his task was made easier. As if royal commanders had not done mischief enough before, Talaban was hampered on this occasion by having two of them set over him, a brother and a son-in-law of the King. Alompra himself took command of the Burmese troops on this occasion, but he was of very different mettle from the royalties at Pegu, and the Talaing army seems to have become panic-stricken at the very thought of encountering him in person. Prome was relieved without much trouble, in January, 1755, but a strong earthwork, which the Talaings had thrown up a few miles south of Prome, was stubbornly defended, and was only taken at the cost of great slaughter on both sides. In this were captured great stores of provisions, of muskets, and of guns a large ship's gun among them. This, from its unwieldiness,

SHWE DAGON PAGODA, RANGOON

Photograph by Mr P. Klier, Rangoon

was of little real use to the Burmese, but it was so highly prized as a trophy that Alompra, though a rigid Buddhist, allowed the gunner, a foreigner, to receive a daily allowance of flesh and of spirits. These were popularly supposed to be offerings to the demon who presided over the fortune of the gun.

From Prome Alompra moved down the river with his army, taking town after town. One of the first to be taken was that which is now known as Myanaung. This word means "speedy victory," and was given by Alompra to the town after he had taken it. Eventually he came to the place where Rangoon now stands. At that time there was no town there, merely the Shwe Dagon pagoda, some monasteries and rest-houses for pilgrims. Here Alompra laid out a new city, which he designed to take the place of Syriam as the chief port of the country. With his usual overwhelming confidence in himself and his love of inspiring names, he named the new port Yangon, which means "Conclusion of the War." This was in May, 1755, at which time the war was by no means over, as Pegu was still in possession of the Talaings, and Syriam was still untaken. All Alompra had done was to subdue the riverine towns from Prome downwards, and a Burmese detachment had taken Bassein and burnt it. It was recaptured by the Talaings, and then taken again by the Burmese.

By this time the Portuguese seem to have no longer been in Burma in any force, but English, French, and Dutch merchants had made their appearance. The Dutch do not seem to have gained any very permanent footing, but the English and French had. As early as 1709 a commercial resident had been appointed by the British Government at Madras to look after the interests of English traders in Burma. Shortly before the rise of Alompra, the island of Negrais had been occupied as a British depôt, by order of the Governor of Madras, apparently without consulting the Government of the country. Subject to this depôt at Negrais there was another at Bassein. At Syriam there was a French as well as a British factory. The French and the English, of course, had no love for each other in Burma any more than in India, and they intrigued in Burma, as in India, to obtain their own ends, by siding with one or other of the native powers. It must often have been very difficult to guess which native potentate it would pay best to side with, and at this juncture the Europeans in Burma must have been sorely puzzled to decide that point. Alompra's rise had been too sudden to inspire confidence, but it is said that at first the French were inclined to side with the Talaings, while the English leaned to the side of the Burmese. Both English and French, however, were far from unanimous in espousing either side, and both were inclined to hedge in a way that must have led the native authorities to think that they were often guilty of treachery. Still they were not so unscrupulous as the Portuguese had been, and Alompra was quite shrewd enough to see that it was better to have them on his side than against him.

When the Burmese first burnt down the town of Bassein, they did no damage to British property there. A month later a Burmese officer arrived at Bassein to communicate with Mr Brooke, the chief of the settlement at Negrais, and to endeavour to procure muskets and gunpowder from him. This Burmese officer went on to Negrais, accompanied by Captain Baker from Bassein. It was during their absence that the Talaings recaptured Bassein, but they were soon driven out by the Burmese, and some military stores were then supplied to the Burmese by Mr Brooke. The chief of the British factory at Syriam had, at first, openly sided with the Burmese, by proceeding with four ships into the Rangoon river, but, later on, when the rains of 1755 had commenced, rendering further action in the delta impracticable, Alompra went to Ava to deal with a threatened rising of the Shan chiefs. No sooner had he gone than the Talaings made an attack on the Burmese camp. It failed, but the British ships, though anchored within gunshot, gave no help to the Burmese. A later attack was made by the Talaings, which was supported by the fire of both the British and the French ships. This obliged the Burmese to abandon their war boats, but nothing tangible resulted. The Talaings retreated to Syriam and both the British and the French ships retired to that port. By siding with the Talaings the officers commanding the British ships at Syriam put Mr Brooke in a very awkward position, as he had sent Captain Baker and Lieutenant North to conclude a treaty with Alompra. At Mutsobomyo, Captain Baker was received by Alompra, and was granted permission to establish factories at Rangoon and Bassein, but Syriam Alompra was determined to destroy. Under all the circumstances of the case it was magnanimous of Alompra to allow English factories at Rangoon and Bassein, but he probably realised that Mr Brooke had not authorised the action on behalf of the Talaings, taken by the officers commanding the British ships, and considered it good policy to keep on good terms with Mr Brooke.

While Mr Brooke, at least, seems from the first almost to have backed the Burmese, M. Bourno, the chief of the French factory at Syriam, tried hedging. Though inclined to support the Talaings, he avoided committing himself definitely to either side. Under pretence of more effectually helping the Talaings, he left Syriam with three ships, and anchored in the Rangoon river. What he saw there led him to believe that it would be better policy to back Alompra, so he proceeded to the royal camp, and was graciously received. During his absence from his ship, the officer left in command, for some unexplained reason, took the vessel back to Syriam. This made Alompra suspicious, but M. Bourno was allowed to depart on his promise to bring back his ship. Later on, as we have seen, both the English and the French ships at Syriam sided with the Talaings against the Burmese. In the case of the British, however, this was done without the sanction of Mr Brooke, the responsible head of the British settlers in Burma. He was away in Negrais, and had no chance of preventing it, but, as M. Bourno was present at Syriam, he could have prevented the French ships from helping the Talaings had he so chosen.

Early in 1756, Alompra returned to Rangoon, and at once took in hand the conquest of Syriam from the Talaings. The British ships had left, but some subordinates were at the factory. One French ship under M. Bourno remained, and was moored close to the factory. When the Burmese army invested the port, the French ship was soon disabled by fire from the Burmese battery. M. Bourno secretly made offers of submission to Alompra, but the Talaing commandant, suspecting treachery, removed the Frenchmen into the port. Alompra took possession of the ship and of the French factory. For several months the port was strictly blockaded, but one rainy night in July, the Burmese forced one of the gates. The garrison, weakened by famine, could make no effectual resistance. The Talaing officers made their escape, but the Europeans, being prisoners, fell into the hands of the conqueror. Two days after the fall of Syriam, a French ship, the Galatée, arrived at the mouth of the river. Alompra compelled M. Bourno to write to the captain to bring his vessel up the river. When she arrived she was seized by the Burmese, and was found to be full of warlike stores. The ship's papers proved that the stores were intended for the King of Pegu. M. Bourno had written some time before to the Governor of Ponticherry urging him to support the King of Pegu, and the Galatée was one of two ships sent in response to this recommendation. Alompra, in his rage at this discovery, put to death, not only M. Bourno, but the captain and officers of the Galatée also. The subordinates of the British factory, who had been put into prison by the Talaings, were now released.

Having conquered Syriam, Alompra next turned his attention to Pegu. As soon as the worst of the rainy season was over, an army of Burmese and Shans settled down round the city. The Talaings knew that their national independence hung on the defence of their capital, and fought with the courage of despair. They made sorties, but by October the outworks were all taken, and Alompra's army had closed round the city. The monks of Pegu then went in a body to the camp of Alompra, and besought him, in the name of religion, to end the war, by allowing the King of Pegu to remain as a tributary king. Alompra's reply was that he would respect existing laws and customs, and that the poor had nothing to fear from him. When the monks came back with this message, Talaban and other Talaing officers represented that submission would mean destruction, so it was resolved to defend the city to the last extremity. By January, 1757, famine had reduced the citizens to the deepest misery, and the council urged the King to offer his daughter to Alompra and again appeal to his mercy.

Talaban protested against this, the princess being betrothed to him, their marriage to take place as soon as he had succeeded in dispersing the Burmese army. He was overborne by the majority of the council, so he determined to leave the city. With his family mounted on elephants, and a devoted band of followers, he managed one night to force his way through the besieging lines, and made good his escape. Then the Talaing King wrote a humble letter to the conqueror, offering his daughter in marriage, and begging to be allowed to remain as a tributary King. According to the Talaing chronicle this offer was accepted, but the Burmese chronicle says the reply merely expressed Alompra's desire to promote the happiness of all beings. To a Talaing officer who accompanied the monk bearing the letter, Alompra presented two bunches of orchid flowers, saying one was an offering and the other for adornment. One bunch was accordingly offered at the great pagoda in Pegu. The other the princess placed in her hair and set off to Alompra's camp, accompanied by a hundred maiden attendants, by the Talaing King's brother and other officers. The latter were retained as hostages, while the princess was received in open court, and, after making obeisance, was conducted to the women's apartments in a palace which Alompra had built outside Pegu.

This somewhat singular marriage seems to have been celebrated with rejoicings, both in Pegu and in the camp of the besiegers, and hostilities were suspended for some days. Then some princesses of the deposed royal family of Ava, whom Alompra was anxious to gain, were allowed to go to him. After this some officers of the Gwe Shans and some Burmese who had taken service with the Talaing King, were surrendered and at once put to death. Alompra next demanded the surrender of the Talaing King's brother, nephew, and son-in-law. This was refused, and some Burmese soldiers who had managed to enter and conceal themselves in Pegu, with instructions to attack the palace on a signal to be given by Alompra, were discovered by the Talaings, and put to death. Things grew worse in the city. Famine became intense, and quarrels broke out among the members of the royal family. Then the wretched King sent secret proposals of surrender, stipulating only that his life should be spared. In the beginning of May, 1757, the Burmese managed to enter by one of the city gates. The houses near the gate were set on fire, and in the general misery and confusion no combined resistance was made. The city was given up to plunder; the conquered King was taken prisoner; most of the leading men, even the monks, according to the Talaing chronicle, were slaughtered; and thousands of men, women and children were sold as slaves.

The fall of Pegu made Alompra practically master of almost all Burma, except Arakan. All the artificers of the city were sent to Mutsobomyo, and the buildings in Pegu were destroyed. Alompra then went down to Rangoon, taking the captive King with him. He appointed a governor to Martaban, and officers to all the districts of the delta, before returning to his own capital. On his way up the Irrawaddy he received in audience Ensign Lester, who had been sent by the chief of the English settlement at Negrais to ask for a treaty of commerce. Alompra commented severely on the action of the British officers at Syriam, but nevertheless, agreed to a treaty, the terms of which were :—

I. Cession to the British of the island of Negrais in perpetuity.

II. Cession of four thousand cubits of ground in Bassein in perpetuity.

III. Free trade.

IV. The East India Company to give the Burmese one 12-pounder and 730 pounds of powder.

V. The Company to defend the King of Burma against all enemies, His Majesty paying the expenses of the troops.

VI. The Company not to assist the King of Tavoy.

This treaty was made in July, 1757, but lasted only about two years. After an expedition to Manipur, in which he found no one to fight, as the Raja and people had all fled to the mountains, Alompra returned to his capital, and began works for bringing in a plentiful supply of water. In the middle of 1759, he had to return to Pegu, as an insurrection had broken out among the Talaings. Rightly or wrongly, the English were suspected of intriguing with the rebels, and, as ill-luck would have it, the "Arcot," one of the British ships which had formerly fired on the Burmese war-boats at Syriam, arrived in Rangoon at this juncture. She had on board Mr Whitehill, who was in the service of the East India Company, and who had been at Rangoon when the "Arcot" fired on the Burmese war-boats. The ship was seized, and Mr Whitehill was sent up to Alompra at Prome. He was treated more leniently, however, than M. Bourno had been, and was allowed to depart on payment of a heavy ransom. Alompra seems then to have had some lingering doubts about the intrigues between the English and Talaings, but on his arrival in Rangoon he received what he considered to be correct information that the agents of the East India Company at Negrais had sold arms and ammunition to the Talaings. He then ordered the settlement to be utterly destroyed. The East India Company, however, had determined to withdraw from Negrais, and from Burma generally, as, at that time, they could not spare the men and money necessary for its effectual support. Part had actually been withdrawn, and in October, 1759, Mr Southby arrived to superintend the establishment still on the island. The following day a sudden attack was made by the Burmese on a building where the Europeans were assembled. Ten of them and nearly a hundred natives of India were murdered. The remaining Indians made good their escape to two British ships in the harbour, while the few Europeans who escaped the massacre were sent as prisoners to Rangoon. It is said that a Frenchman helped in the massacre of the English, and that a Portuguese, named Antony, in the pay of the Burmese Government, gave the signal for it to commence, by withdrawing when all the English officers had assembled in the building, where a dinner was being given, apparently in honour of Mr Southby's arrival.

Alompra's next move was to invade Siam. The King of that country had refused, it is stated, to give him one of his daughters in marriage. Moreover, thousands of Talaings had taken refuge in Siam, and bands of that race had made incursions on the Tavoy frontier, which had lately been re-occupied by the Burmese. His principal officers endeavoured to dissuade him, and the astrologers predicted disaster, but Alompra would not listen. He set off in December, 1759, overcame all opposition on the way, and by April, 1760, took up a position before the capital, Ayuthia. The Siamese King remained on the defensive, expecting the enemy to retire when the river rose and flooded their camp. Alompra found he could not maintain his army during a prolonged siege, so he resorted to guile. He declared that he had come, as a future Buddha, to preach the law of holiness. The Siamese were not to be deceived by so obvious a falsehood, so they ridiculed his pretentions and defied his power. At this juncture Alompra became very ill, from the effects of an abscess, so a retreat was ordered. The dying King was carried in a litter, and the retreating army was greatly harassed by the Siamese. When half way to the Salween, Alompra died, at the age of forty-six. The body was conveyed to the capital, and was there burnt, with the funeral rites of a Chakravarti or universal monarch. His career had certainly been a remarkable one. In eight years he had risen from the position of an obscure official, under a regime which had totally collapsed, to that of the monarch of the greater part of Burma. Force of character and ability he must have had, but he had also an overwhelming confidence in himself, which, in the end, led even him to disaster. His successors had, for the most part, his conceit in full measure, but without his ability, so they went from disaster to disaster. One drastic lesson after another failed to bring home to their minds any perception of their own limitations.

CHAPTER VIII.

A.D. 1760 TO 1784

ALOMPRA, before his death, had expressed the wish that his six sons by his first wife should succeed him in the order of their seniority. Accordingly, the eldest, who had remained at the capital as regent during the ill-fated expedition to Siam, ascended the throne under the name of Naungdawgyi. When the son of Alompra who had accompanied the expedition to Siam, left to take his father's body to Mutsobomyo, the command of the army fell to a trusted officer of Alompra, named Noratha. This man seems to have thought that the circumstances gave him a chance of making a bid for the throne himself. He first made a futile attempt on Taungu, where Alompra's brother was governor; there an attempt was made to arrest him, but he escaped, marched to Ava, expelled the governor, and occupied that city. This was in June, 1760, only about a month after Alompra's death. King Naungdawgyi promptly marched on Ava and closely invested the city. All attacks were repulsed by the garrison, and it was not until December that Noratha recognised the hopelessness of his position. Famine had made surrender inevitable, so he fled with a few horsemen, but was shot before he got very far.

During the siege of Ava, Captain Alves appeared at Sagaing, where King Naungdawgyi was, bringing letters from the Madras Government demanding redress for the massacre at Negrais. Captain Alves had commanded one of the English ships anchored off Negrais when the massacre occurred. He was admitted to an audience, but was treated with great indignity, and all compensation was peremptorily refused, on the ground that Mr Whitehill and the governor of Negrais were the aggressors, while Mr Southby, who had just arrived, and could not have committed any offence, was included with the rest " just as herbs are consumed with the weeds when, ground is cleared by burning." All King Naungdawgyi would do was to liberate the English prisoners and give a grant of land for a factory at Bassein. At a later interview he asked what personal favour Captain Alves would like to have conferred on him, and at once conceded the request made, namely, that three Dutchmen, who had been captured in Siam, should be liberated.

In 1761, the King's uncle, who governed Taungu, fell under suspicion. He failed to obey a summons to submit himself, so the King marched with an army to bring him to obedience. During the siege of Taungu, Talaban, who was now in the service of the King of Zimmè, entered Martaban with a considerable force, and, for a time, threatened an attack on the besieging army. As soon as Taungu was taken, in January, 1762, the King ordered a march to Zimmè. The expedition was successful, and the capital of that state was occupied without difficulty. Talaban, his wife, and family, were captured, and it is generally believed that he was put to death, though the Burmese chronicle says that his life was spared. Naungdawgyi then devoted himself to the erection of religious buildings, but died suddenly in November, 1763. His reign was very short, but he seems to have been capable enough, and to have governed well, according to his lights. He was an ardent Buddhist, and punished by death, drunkenness and the slaughter of animals for food. It was a curious way of interpreting the Buddhist precepts against any taking of life.

Alompra's second son then ascended the throne, under the title Sinbyushin, which means "Lord of the White Elephant." In 1764 he conquered Manipur, and put one of his own relatives on the throne there, bringing back to Burma much treasure and many prisoners. His next endeavour was to avenge the failure of his father in Siam. Two armies were despatched thither by different routes; these overcame all opposition on the way, and by the beginning of 1766, they met and invested the Siamese capital, Ayuthia. The Siamese King adopted the old tactics of remaining on the defensive and trusting to the floods dispersing the enemy. When the river did rise the Burmese were in a sorry plight, but they maintained their ground in small parties on the more elevated portions of ground. After the rains were over, the Burmese again constructed earthworks, and, as all supplies were cut off, the position of the besieged became hopeless. After an ineffectual attempt to escape, the Siamese King offered to become a tributary, but the Burmese would accept nothing short of unconditional surrender. Eventually the city was taken, the King was killed, and his family taken prisoners. The amount of treasure and stores taken was considerable. Arrangements were made for Siam to be ruled as a tributary state, and the Burmese army returned to Ava in 1767.

An incident occurred during the siege of Ayuthia which is interesting, as showing the position of the English at that time. An English captain, named Powny, arrived with a cargo of general merchandise, and bringing a lion, an Arab horse, and some goods for the King of Siam. The latter asked him to undertake the defence of the city, but he refused, as he had reason to believe from the past experience of the Dutch and Portuguese settlers there, that he would not be properly supported by the Siamese soldiers. Captain Powny retired to Bangkok, where he was attacked by the Burmese. He then decided to help the Siamese, and, as a pledge of fidelity, he deposited thirty-eight bales of valuable cargo in the public magazine. The fire from his ship destroyed the earthworks of the enemy and did considerable damage to them. He then asked for more arms and ammunition to enable him to disperse the Burmese, but the Siamese were suspicious and refused to comply with this demand. Captain Powny then left them to their own devices, and sailed away in disgust. Before doing so, however, he seized a Chinese vessel which was laden on the King's account, and from this and five others, which he also captured, he was able to indemnify himself for his losses in the King's service. To the captains of these vessels he gave bills drawn on the King of Siam to the value of the thirty-eight bales deposited in the public magazine. The Burmese were delighted at his departure, but the Siamese had every reason to regret their suspiciousness, for they were totally defeated, and their capital laid in ruins.

Almost all the Kings of the Alompra dynasty started a new capital for the country. Alompra himself had made Mutsobomyo his capital, which is intelligible enough, as it was his own birthplace. His successors, however, instead of retaining it as the capital, kept constantly shifting the seat of government. Naungdawgyi made Sagaing his capital, and his successor, Sinbyushin, shifted the capital back to Ava. It was a most inconvenient arrangement, entailing great hardship on the people, numbers of whom had always to follow the court from one capital to another.

While the war with Siam was in progress, misunderstandings arose between Burma and China. In 1765 a Chinese merchant, wishing to take his merchandise across the Taping river, asked the governor of Bhamo for leave to build a bridge. Resenting the delay in obtaining a reply, he used some expressions which the Burmese officials considered abusive. He was then sent as a prisoner to Ava, but was released and sent back with the necessary permission to build the bridge. Meantime some of his goods had disappeared, and the governor of Bhamo rejected his claim for compensation. He then reported the matter to the governor of Yunnan. Another Chinese trader at Kyanton, failing to obtain payment for goods sold, a quarrel arose in which a Chinaman was killed. The Burmese officials offered money compensation, but nothing short of giving up the manslayer, or a substitute, would satisfy the Chinese. This grievance was also reported to the governor of Yunnan. The result was no fewer than four Chinese expeditions into Burma between December, 1765, and December, 1769. In these the Burmese soldiers seem to have been quite able to hold their own, their success being largely due to the superiority of their artillery, which according to Father Sangermano, was "served by the Christians, who had established themselves in these parts." These Christians were the descendants of Portuguese and French captives.

Meantime, the Siamese had thrown off the Burmese yoke. A man of Chinese descent, and a distant relative of the deposed King, had established his capital at Bangkok, and had brought some of the adjacent country into subjection. In 1771 Sinbyushin sent an army to deal with Siam, but at the first reverse met with, the Martaban division, consisting of Talaings, broke into open rebellion. Sinbyushin thereupon went down the river to Rangoon, travelling in great state, and bringing the deposed Talaing King in his train. He also brought a new *htee* for the Shwe Dagon pagoda. The replacing the old *htee* by a new one brought from Ava was intended to have a political significance for the Talaings, and, to drive the lesson home to them, their former King was tried on a charge of having instigated the recent rebellion. The charge was false and the trial a mockery, but the ex-king was brought in guilty, sentenced to death, and met his death at the hands of the public executioner, in 1775. Several other Talaing notables shared his fate. Another expedition was sent to Siam, but dissensions broke out among the officers and men, and after a defeat at the hands of the Siamese, the army returned to Burma.

Sinbyushin died in 1776, shortly after his return to Ava, and then ensued a struggle for the throne. Instead of adhering to Alompra's directions about the succession, a court intrigue managed to put Sinbyushin's son on the throne. This lad of nineteen was singularly unfit for the position, but a court faction often prefers a successor of this age, as being likely to prove a pliable tool in their hands for a few years at least. They object to a child because the succession of a child involves the appointment of a regent, who would not be any more pliable than a successor of mature years. But a lad of eighteen or nineteen is not supposed to need a regent, and yet may prove to be easily managed by astute court officials, skilled in flattery. Poor Singu Min, the lad chosen in this case, seems to have been a poor creature. He made no effort to retrieve the defeat in Siam. Feeling his own position insecure, he put his uncle, Alompra's fourth son, to death; he brought about the death of his own younger brother, and in a fit of anger drowned his favourite wife. After these amiable attentions to his relatives, he took to making pilgrimages to distant pagodas; not so much, apparently, from any feeling of remorse, as because life in the palace with nothing to do had become monotonous and tiresome to him. This lad reigned, if such an existence can be called "reigning," for five years, but in 1781 another plot was hatched and another lad of eighteen was put upon the throne. This was the son of Naungdawgyi, Alompra's eldest son. He had been a mere infant at the time of his father's death in 1763, but was now eighteen, and if Alompra's younger sons were to be thrown out of the succession, and if seniority was to count as a claim, though practically it counts for very little in Burma, this lad, as the son of Alompra's eldest son, had a better claim than Singu Min. Anyway, during one of Singu Min's pilgrimages, this lad was brought into the palace and proclaimed King. What happened to Singu Min is not certainly known. One account is that when he returned to the palace he was cut down by the father of the wife whom he had drowned in a fit of rage.

The boy put on the throne this time only kept his seat for eleven days. Then the fifth son of Alompra ousted him and seized the throne, taking the name Bodopra. He started his reign by killing all those who had been implicated in putting his immediate predecessor on the throne. This led to several conspiracies against him, one of which nearly succeeded, but Bodopra overcame them all, and exacted a terrible vengeance in the case of the conspirator who was nearly successful. This man had been killed with all his followers in the struggle, but Bodopra, not satisfied with this, completely destroyed the village to which he had belonged, burning the majority of its inhabitants, men, women, children, and even the monks, on an immense pile of wood. This atrocity was enacted in December, 1782. Another Talaing rebellion had broken out near Rangoon, but this was crushed, and five hundred of the rebels were executed in public as a warning to others. While Bodopra was securing his throne by such drastic measures as these, he had also been building a new capital six miles from Ava. Of this he took formal possession in 1783, naming it Amarapura, or the City of Immortals.

For long Arakan had lain outside the struggles going on in Burma. During all that time its history is more nearly connected with that of India than with that of Burma. But Bodopra now turned his attention to it. He had been invited to interfere immediately after his accession in 1781, as by this time Arakan was in a state of anarchy. But Bodopra was shrewd enough to see that his first task must be to secure his power in the territories Alompra had won. It was not till 1784 that he was able to send an army into Arakan, and then he despatched a well-equipped expedition, under the command of his eldest son. Part of this army went by the passes over the Yomadaung chain, while the remainder went along the coast by sea. In the distracted state of Arakan, it was easy to overthrow such government as existed. The King, the queens, and the principal officials, were taken as captives to Amarapura, and a very celebrated large image of Guadama, known as the *Mahamuni* was dragged across the Taungup pass and brought to the Burmese capital. A garrison of ten thousand Burmese soldiers was located in Arakan, under a Burmese governor, but a number of Arakanese, rather than submit to Burmese rule, fled to Chittagong, and settled among the hills. The incorporation of Arakan in the kingdom of Burma was a very natural ambition for the King of Burma; but it brought the Burmese empire into touch with the rapidly growing British power in India, and so precipitated a conflict which would, however, have been inevitable in any case, sooner or later. Neither Bodopra, nor any of his successors ever realised the strength of the power which had now become their neighbour, and their overwhelming conceit led them to misunderstand any forbearance shown to them by the Government of India, and to meet every attempt at a friendly mutual understanding with arrogant rudeness and bluster. The circumstances were so completely changed by the conquest of Arakan, which was finally completed by the end of 1784, that it will be best to continue the account of Bodopra's reign in another chapter.

CHAPTER IX.

A.D. 1785 TO 1819

BODOPRA was far from realising what the conquest of Arakan involved, and, no sooner was this completed than he started ambitious projects in other directions. In 1785 he sent a land force and eleven ships under officers of Portuguese descent to take the island of Junkseylon, then in the possession of Siam. The fort on the island was taken, the Siamese governor retreating to the interior of the island. A ship belonging to a Mahomedan merchant was chartered to convey the spoil to Rangoon, but met with a storm in the Gulf of Martaban, and was lost. In the island, the Siamese governor rallied his forces and drove off the Burmese, who returned to Mergui. The next few years were spent in struggles with Siam, with very varying results. The Burmese invaded Siam, and the Siamese invaded Burma, the various struggles resulting at one time in a victory for the Burmese and at another time in their defeat. One unfortunate Burmese commander who had been defeated by the Siamese, was sent back in chains and publicly executed by order of Bodopra. The net result of all this fighting with Siam was a treaty concluded in 1793, in which the Siamese waived all claims to Tavoy, Mergui, and Tenasserim. It was a result very far short of what the Burmese Kings had long aimed at, namely the total conquest of Siam.

Meantime, in Arakan, things were not progressing satisfactorily. Oppression and heavy exactions drove the Arakanese to repeated insurrections, and numbers fled to Chittagong. In 1793 three insurgent Arakanese chiefs fled into British territory. A Burmese general, with five thousand men crossed the Naf and demanded their surrender. He fortified his camp with a stockade, and awaited compliance with his demand. Sir John Shore, then Governor-General of India, sent a force, under General Erskine to compel the Burmese to withdraw. No actual engagement took place, however, as in an interview between the two commanders, the Burmese officer consented to withdraw on the assurance that enquiry would be made into the charges brought against the fugitives. They were charged with rebellion, robbery and murder. They were rebels, of course, from the Burmese point of view, and active rebellion is apt to involve both murder and robbery. The result of the enquiry was that the three chiefs were given up, and two of them were executed. The episode is not altogether creditable to the Government of India, but some allowance must be made, as affairs in India itself were amply sufficient to demand all the available resources, and Government was sincerely anxious to avoid, if possible, being drawn into Burmese affairs. It had ample to do at home, and would only have been too thankful to leave Burma alone.

In the hope of coming to some friendly understanding with the Burmese Government, Captain Symes of H.M. 76th Regiment, was sent on a mission to Amarapura, with presents for the King, and a letter from Sir John Shore. Captain Symes arrived in Rangoon on the 20th March, but was detained there on various pretexts for fully two months. When he reached Amarapura, on 17th July, a common mat house was given to him to live in, but he was not received by the King until the beginning of September. Bodopra took no notice of the presents or of the letter from the Governor-General. The only privilege he accorded was the permission to appoint a British Consul in Rangoon. In spite of the indignities to which their envoy had been subjected, the Government of India sent Captain Cox to Rangoon as Consul in 1796. He had an interview with the King at Amarapura, but was treated with greater indignity than Captain Symes had been. The officers of the mission were pelted with stones by the mob, and when they returned to Rangoon, the Governor of Pegu refused to allow them to leave Burma. Captain Cox had to remain until 1798, and to endure many humiliations during his stay in Rangoon.

Meantime the Arakanese were emigrating in thousands into British territory, to escape from Burmese rule. There was not even the pretext in this case that they had been guilty of open rebellion. They merely preferred British to Burmese rule, so crossed the frontier into Chittagong. But the King of Burma objected to losing his subjects wholesale in this way. They were his property, he considered, and should be made to stay in his territory, whether they wished to or not. A Burmese detachment was again sent beyond the Naf to demand their surrender, but this was withdrawn, and an envoy sent to Calcutta to negotiate for the surrender of the fugitives. Lord Wellesley was now Governor-General, and he refused to give up the fugitives, but he undertook that they should not be allowed to molest the Burmese in Arakan. This was reasonable enough, but he undertook also that in future no others would be allowed to cross into British territory. Practically this amounted to denying a refuge to the oppressed still in Arakan, but the Government of India had still quite enough to do in India, and was most anxious to keep out of Burma. In order to settle the matter more satisfactorily, Captain Symes was again sent, in 1802, to try to come to a friendly understanding with the King. On 30th September, he arrived at Mingun, where the King was. For about forty days he was utterly unnoticed, and was compelled to live on an unhealthy island in the river all the time. Then he received a verbal message to the effect that the King would make no treaty, would allow no commercial privileges, and would not permit any British Resident to be stationed in Rangoon or Amarapura.

In spite of all these rebuffs, Captain Canning was sent in 1809 with a letter and presents for the King. He reached the capital on 10th February, 1810, and was received in audience on the 28th. The King expressed the wish that an ambassador should be sent to him direct from the King of England. A few days later, Captain Canning received a letter addressed to Lord Wellesley, in which the restoration of Dacca and Chittagong to the Burmese was hinted at, and the remark made that the Governor-General should always consider himself under the protection of the King of Burma. On this occasion there was less discourtesy to the envoy, but Bodopra's opinion of his own claims had greatly increased, and his pretensions become altogether preposterous.

Captain Canning returned to Calcutta in April, 1810, but it was not long before he had to return to Burma to explain an episode in which the English appeared to be in the wrong, and actually were so to the extent that they had failed, in one instance, at least, to prevent a refugee in Chittagong from heading an insurrection against Burmese authority in Arakan. A man named Khyinbran had lived quietly in Chittagong for some years, but in 1811 he headed an insurrection in Arakan, secured the town of Arakan, and reduced a considerable tract of country to his authority. He was soon, however, defeated by the Burmese, and took refuge again in British territory. The Burmese governor of Arakan was convinced that Khyinbran had been encouraged by the British officials in Chittagong. This was not the case, of course, as the British were only too anxious to avoid being drawn into hostilities with Burma, but it was natural that the Burmese authorities should think otherwise. Captain Canning was sent to disavow all connection with the insurgents, and to assure the King of the Indian Government's desire to be on friendly terms with him. When Captain Canning reached Rangoon, the governor determined to detain him as a hostage for the delivery of Khyinbran, but this was frustrated by the presence in Rangoon of two armed cruisers in the service of the East India Company. He returned to Bengal in August, 1812. As to Khyinbran, he seems to have outwitted both the British and the Burmese authorities, and to have continued to harass the Burmese in Arakan until his death in the early part of 1815.

In 1818, the Raja of Ramri, an island on the Arakan coast, took it upon himself to send an insolent letter to the Governor-General, demanding the cession to the Burmese of Chittagong, Murshedabad and Dacca, as being dependencies of the kingdom of Arakan. This elicited the first really firm and dignified reply in the dealings of the Government of India with Burma. The Marquis of Hastings sent the letter to the Viceroy of Pegu, with an expression of his belief that it was an unauthorised document, and an intimation that, had it come from the King of Burma, it would have amounted to a declaration of war.

While there was thus constant friction on the Arakanese frontier, various missions were sent by the Burmese King to India. The ostensible object of all thes missions was to make offerings at Buddha Gaya, and to procure sacred relics and holy books. The Government of India, apparently, accepted the avowed religious character of these missions in all good faith, and they were allowed to penetrate into all parts of India. But it was discovered later that the missions were not wholly taken up with the pious designs they put forward. Bodopra was scheming to join in any confederacy of Indian princes which might be formed to resist the British. The British and Burmese Governments were at cross purposes right through. The British Government of India would have left Burma severely alone had Bodopra confined his energies to his own territory, but he was bent on entering into the welter of Indian politics, with which he had no real concern at all. It was partly, no doubt, because he feared the British power, which he believed to be guilty of fomenting trouble in Arakan. But it was partly also due to the overwhelming conceit which led him, along with others of the Alompra dynasty, to believe themselves almost more than human. It is a form of conceit that goes very near madness. For instance, when a mission from Ceylon, or at least professing to represent that island, entreated him to revive religion, now desolated by foreign heretics, he replied that he intended to follow the example of "his great ancestor, Asoka." The answer was as preposterous as if a modern Christian sovereign were to say that he meant to follow the example of "his great ancestor, King David." Asoka had been dead for some two thousand years, he was of a different race altogether, and had never had any connection with Burma, except, perhaps, to the extent of sending some Buddhist missionaries there.

Bodopra did execute some works of public utility. Among them was the enlargement of an old tank, a few miles to the north-east of Amarapura. The enlarged reservoir of about twenty square miles was capable of holding sufficient water to irrigate several thousand acres of land. It was named *Aungpinle*, or "The Enclosed Sea." It is a pity he did not confine himself to the construction of such reservoirs, which are sadly needed in the dry zone, but he conceived the idea that he should build a bigger pagoda than anyone else had ever achieved. The site chosen was at Mingun, and there a huge mass of brickwork remains to this day, in mockery of this ambitious scheme. There also is still to be seen the huge bell, weighing eighty tons, which was cast for this pagoda. The King was so bent on this work that he had a temporary palace built, and lived at Mingun to superintend the work. The building of this pagoda must have been a terrible tax on the King's subjects, but it was persevered in for twenty years. Even then it had only been raised to about a third of the proposed height, but the King abandoned it. One reason given is that a prophecy had been circulated to the effect that the King's life would end with the completion of the structure. If this story is true, it is an excellent illustration of the way in which a despot can sometimes be turned from his purpose. Any reasoning or any appeals to his pity would have been quite useless, but to suggest that his own life would end when the work was completed, was a happy thought, and secured the release of the unfortunate workers at once. The mass of brickwork remains to this day, a huge memorial of human vanity and folly.

GREAT BELL AT MINGUN PAGODA

Photograph by Mr Samuels, Mandalay

It does not even stand as Bodopra left it when he died in 1819, as twenty years after his death, the mass of brickwork was shattered to its foundation by an earthquake.

Father Sangermano, an Italian priest, lived in Burma for twenty years during Bodopra's reign. He arrived in 1783, and went directly to Ava, but afterwards returned to Rangoon and engaged in missionary work there. He built the Church of St. John, where St. John's Convent now stands, and he superintended a college where Burmese lads were educated. After his return to Europe he wrote a "Description of the Burmese Empire," the following extracts from which will give some idea of what he thought of the Burmese system of government, and of King Bodopra in particular.

"I suppose that there is not in the whole world a monarch so despotic as the Burmese Emperor. He is considered, by himself and others, absolute lord of the lives, properties, and personal services of his subjects; he exalts and depresses, confers and takes away honour and rank; and, without any process of law, can put to death, not only criminals guilty of capital offences, but any individual who happens to incur his displeasure. It is here a perilous thing for a person to become distinguished for wealth and possessions; for the day may easily come when he will be charged with some supposed crime, and so put to death, in order that his property may be confiscated. Every subject is the Emperor's born slave; and when he calls anyone his slave he thinks thereby to do him honour. To express their sense of this subjection, all who approach him are obliged to prostrate themselves before him, holding their hands joined above their heads. Hence, also, he considers himself entitled to employ his subjects in any work or service, without salary or pay, and if he makes them any recompense, it is done, not from a sense of justice, but as an act of bounty. Their goods, likewise, and even their persons are reputed his property, and on this ground it is that he selects for his concubine any female that may chance to please his eye. . . . .

" Although despotism in its worst form constitutes, as it were, the very essence of the Burmese monarchy, so that to be called its King is equivalent to being called a tyrant ; still has Badonsachen (Bodopra), the despot who for the last twenty-seven years has governed this kingdom, so far outstripped his predecessors in barbarity and pride, that whoso but hears of it must shudder with horror. His very countenance is the index of a mind, ferocious and inhuman in the highest degree, and what has been above related of him, as well as some more facts to be brought forward, will show that it does not deceive. Immense is the number of those whom he has sacrificed to his ambition, upon the most trivial offences ; and it would not be an exaggeration to assert that, during his reign, more victims have fallen by the hand of the executioner than by the hand of the common enemy. To this atrocious cruelty he has united a pride at once intolerable and impious. The good fortune which has attended him in discovering and defeating the numerous conspiracies which have been formed against him, has inspired him with the idea that he is something more than mortal, and that this privilege has been granted him on account of his numerous good works. Hence has he, for some years, laid aside the title of King, and assumed that of Pondoghi, which signifies great and exalted virtue ; nor was he content with this, for but a few years since he thought to make himself a God. With this view, and in imitation of Godama, who, before

MINGUN PAGODA

Photograph by Mr Samuels, Mandalay

being advanced to the rank of a divinity, had abandoned the royal palace, together with all his wives and concubines, and had retired into solitude, Badonsachen withdrew himself from the palace to Menton (Mingun), where for many years he had been employed in constructing a pagoda, the largest in the empire. Here he held various conferences with the most considerable and learned Talapoins (monks), in which he endeavoured to persuade them, that the five thousand years assigned for the observance of the law of Godama were elapsed, and that he himself was the God, who was to appear after that period, and to abolish the ancient law in substituting his own. But to his great mortification, many of the Talapoins undertook to demonstrate the contrary; and this, combined with his love of power and his impatience under the denial of the luxuries of the seraglio, quickly disabused him of his Godhead, and drove him back to his palace."

The good Father then gives the form of address which was presented to an ambassador from the Governor-General of India to be pronounced by him before the Burmese King. " Placing above our heads the golden majesty of the mighty lord, the possessor of the mines of rubies, amber, gold, silver and all kinds of metals; of the lord under whose command are innumerable soldiers, generals and captains; of the lord who is King of many countries and provinces, and emperor over many rulers and princes, who wait round his throne with the badges of his authority; of the lord who is adorned with the greatest power, wisdom, knowledge, prudence, foresight, etc.; of the lord who is rich in the possession of elephants and horses, and in particular is the lord of many white elephants; of the lord who is greatest of Kings, the most just and the most religious, the master of life and death; we, his slaves, the Governor of Bengal, the officers and administrators of the Company, bowing and lowering our heads under the sole of his royal golden foot, do present to him, with the greatest veneration, this our humble petition."

Father Sangermano goes on to describe the oppression of the people. " As the reigning monarch has had more than a hundred children by his numerous wives and concubines, they have swallowed all the riches of the land; the cities, villages and lakes have been almost all given them for their maintenance; and the best situations, as of Vunghi and of the Lutto, have been distributed among them." Then, on the river, which, in the absence of all roads, was the great highway, numerous toll-houses, which the Italian Father calls cioché, were placed to exact dues from every passing boat. " Foreigners in particular are exposed to the rapacity of the exactors, and unfortunate, indeed, is he, who is so imprudent as to embark his goods for Amarapura. The visits of the inspectors resemble a robbery rather than a collection of dues; for besides the usual tax, so much is demanded under the name of presents, and so much is stolen, that the owner, after having passed two or three cioché, will generally be glad to hasten back to Rangoon, rather than try the mercy of future plunderers. This, in fact, did happen a short time since to some foreign merchants. But the extortions and oppressions of which I have just spoken, are nothing in comparison to those practised by the Mandarins in the provincial cities, and above all, in Rangoon. For this city, being situated at a great distance from the court, is more exposed to their rapacity; and being the principal sea-port of the kingdom, where numbers of foreigners flock with their merchandise, the inhabitants have more opportunities of gain, and thus furnish a richer harvest for the avarice of their rulers. The Emperor gives no salary to the Mandarins ; indeed, before any one can obtain the dignity, he must spend large sums in presents, and in order to maintain himself in it, still larger ones are necessary, not only to the Emperor, but also to his queens, and to all the principal personages about the court. To this must be added the expenses of these grandees in their houses, dress and equipages, which must be proportionable to their dignity ; and when we consider that the money for all this must be furnished by the people under their care, it will easily be imagined what dreadful oppression is put in practice to draw it from them."

These extracts give an excellent account from an intelligent eye-witness of what Burma was towards the close of the eighteenth century. The same system had, doubtless, prevailed for centuries before. It certainly did continue for nearly a century longer in those parts of the country that remained under native rule. Even when the King was a fairly good one, he could do little to check the abuses of this system. The officials received no salary, they had to bribe to obtain their place, and they had to send remittances to the capital. So long as these came up to the amount expected, no questions were asked as to how the money had been raised. The official raised as much as he could by fair means or foul, and kept as much as he dared for himself. Trade was strangled by the numerous exactions, so there was little chance of any non-official acquiring wealth. If any one did so, he was careful to conceal the fact, otherwise he was liable to be bled by the nearest person in authority. The man desiring a quiet life was safest in a monastery. If he objected to being a monk, he, at least, had to appear poor, and generally was so, as a matter of fact, as there was no inducement to acquire wealth. The ambitious became officials, and often acquired wealth, but even they held their wealth by a very precarious tenure, as they made numerous enemies, and if one of these gained the ear of the King, the highest official might at any moment lose his wealth and his head too.

Father Sangermano is, perhaps, a little too hard on King Bodopra, especially in the matter of his impiety. To set himself up as a Buddha was a very different thing from a Christian setting himself up as God. Guadama was a man who found the way of enlightenment for himself and for those who would follow his teaching. There have been Buddhas before Guadama, and there will be Buddhas after him, so there is no very great impiety in anyone imagining himself to be a future Buddha. Alompra had called himself the embryo Buddha, and to any Buddhist this aspiration is not impious. Bodopra's impiety was rather a colossal conceit, which impelled him to believe that he was already on the point of Buddha-hood, though only half the period of five thousand years assigned for the observance of Guadama's law had expired, and though his own life of self-indulgence, to say nothing of the number of persons he had condemned to death, was the very antithesis of the life anyone aspiring to Buddha-hood must lead. There he showed the conceit that runs near madness, but the circumstances of his life were enough to turn any but the strongest head. He is said to have been forty-six years of age when he came to the throne in 1781. If so, he was a lad of eighteen when his father began to emerge from obscurity, just the age when he would be most liable to be dazzled by the family's wonderful rise into power. Yet during the following twenty-eight years which elapsed before he came to the throne himself, he must have walked with considerable circumspection and prudence, more especially after the accession of Sinbyushin's son. This lad did kill one of his uncles as the surest method of getting rid of an inconvenient rival. Bodopra had just as good a claim to the throne as the other son of Alompra who was killed, yet his life was spared. It is evident that he must have lain low at that time, probably in a monastery. During part of his life he was a monk, and when the succession laid down by Alompra was departed from, his safest place would certainly be a monastery.

Whatever Bodopra's faults of character may have been, he can scarcely have been quite the monster Father Sangermano pictures. The life of a possible rival for the throne in Burma is always somewhat precarious, and liable to be forfeited for any indiscretion. Bodopra succeeded in avoiding the dangers of that period, and made no bid for the throne until he saw his way to secure it effectually. When he had done that, there is no doubt that he did some cruel things, but he had to strike terror into the hearts of those who engineered the conspiracies against him. During thirty-eight years, from 1781 to 1819, he not only kept together the kingdom he had inherited, but added to it the long-lost province of Arakan. He must have been over eighty when he died, but to the last he seems to have administered the country with firmness. His character was not altogether admirable. After some years of successful kingship he seems to have acquired an insane pride, and his methods of putting down disorder seem to us needlessly brutal; but, at least, he was no weakling, and he held the empire together as no weakling could have done. Under a weakling the empire would have gone to pieces again, and the resulting chaos would have produced more misery and more deaths than even Bodopra's iron rule produced. His religion was probably sincere enough, and his public works on a large scale were quite in keeping with the teachings of Buddhism. Much of the rest of his life was not, no doubt, but rigid adherence to Buddhist teaching is only possible to a monk. Bodopra died at Amarapura, in May, 1819, and Father Sangermano, who has left such an unflattering account of him, died during the same year in his native Italy.

CHAPTER X.

A.D. 1819 TO 1826

THE death of a Burmese King, especially of one leaving about a hundred children, as Bodopra did, is apt to result in a scramble for the throne, and much killing of his brothers by the one who succeeds in seizing it. Bodopra seems always to have taken what measures he could to prevent the occurrence of this on his own death. His eldest son had been appointed heir-apparent, and when he died, his son succeeded to the title. The result of this settlement of the succession, years beforehand, was that the heir-apparent, Bodopra's grandson, succeeded without opposition. He was thirty-seven years of age at the time, and took the name Bagyidaw. Though the Burmese are apt to think that sons should come before grandsons, all Bagyidaw's uncles, except two, seem to have acquiesced in his succession. The two exceptions were the Princes of Prome and Taungu, who started a conspiracy some weeks later, or were supposed to have done so. For this, they and a large number of their adherents were put to death.

The Rajah of Manipur had for some time shown symptoms of a disposition to throw off the suzerainty of Burma, and, on Bagyidaw's accession, he made excuses for not coming in to pay homage to the new sovereign. An expedition was accordingly sent to Manipur at the end of 1819 to bring him to reason. The expedition was successful, but is specially remarkable, as it was in this campaign that Maha Bundula, afterwards a very famous Burmese general, first attracted attention. The ruler of Assam next tried to throw off the Burmese yoke, but Bundula defeated him also, in 1822, and Assam then became a Burmese province, the ruler taking refuge in British territory. In the same year a great fire broke out in Amarapura, and a vulture alighted on the spire of the palace. The astrologers declared that these portents foreboded evil, so the capital was again changed to Ava.

The British had not been very willing to let the Burmese annex Assam, and had given the ruler arms and ammunition to enable him to resist the Burmese; but when this failed, they accepted the accomplished fact. They, however, specially warned the Burmese that they would not tolerate interference in Cachar. That province they had taken under their protection, so that the passes into Sylhet could be occupied, and any advance of the Burmese thereby, from the north and east, effectually checked. In spite of this warning, two Burmese armies, one from Manipur and the other from Assam, marched into Cachar, and in January, 1824, the first conflict between the British and Burmese took place. The British force consisted of a battalion of sepoys under Colonel Bowen. In the first encounter the Burmese were defeated, but, the Burmese being reinforced, Colonel Bowen had to retire before superior numbers. The Burmese then pushed on and threw up entrenchments on the banks of the Surma. They were driven from there and the Assam column returned home, while that from Manipur retired to a strong stockade on the Barak river. Colonel Bowen failed in an attempt to storm this stockade, but the Burmese soon after abandoned the position and returned to Manipur.

Meantime there was constant trouble on the Chittagong frontier. In 1821 and 1822, elephant parties were seized by the Burmese, and only set free on payment of a ransom. In 1823, the Burmese claimed the right to levy tolls on all boats entering the Naf. On one occasion a boat on the British side of the river was fired upon, and the steersman killed. In the same year the island of Shapuri, or Sinbyugyun, was attacked by one thousand Burmans. Three sepoys were killed, four wounded, and the rest of the guard was driven off. The commander of a pilot vessel in the Chittagong service was treacherously seized, along with another officer, and the two were sent as prisoners to Arakan.

It was now quite evident that forbearance and conciliation were useless; were taken only as a sign of fear, and that they only encouraged the Burmese in arrogance and bombastic pride. It was known in Calcutta that one of the Burmese generals had announced his intention of taking possession of that town on his way to England! There was no course open but to prove to the Burmese that there were limits to British forbearance, and that the British could attack if necessary as well as act on the defensive. Accordingly, on the 5th of March, 1824, an official declaration of war was issued by the Government of Fort William. Troops were sent into Assam under the command of Colonel McMorine, but the Burmese withdrew and left him in quiet possession of the country. In Chittagong, however, the British force was far too small for the work that fell to it. In January, 1824, Bundula left Ava with a picked body of six thousand men to take command in Arakan. He crossed into that province by the Aeng pass, and in May he sent a body of four thousand men across the Naf, to attack the British force stationed at Ramu. Captain

Noton, who commanded this force, had only three hundred and fifty regulars, six hundred and fifty police, and a levy of Arakanese refugees, to oppose to the Burmese. The result was a total defeat of the British, Captain Noton and most of his brother officers being slain in the engagement. This action was fought on 17th May, 1824. When the news of it reached Calcutta, it was supposed that the Burmese would at once advance on that town, as there was no intermediate force to oppose their advance. In this emergency, the European inhabitants formed themselves into a militia, and a large proportion of the crews of the ships in the harbour was landed to help in the defence of the town. The commander of the Burmese force, however, referred to Bundula for instructions before making any further advance, and the latter, probably realising that his services would soon be required nearer home, determined not to follow up the success at Ramu, but to bring the Burmese force back again across the Naf into Arakan. This caution on his part seems to show that he, himself, did not quite believe the boasts he used to indulge in. It is said that he took to Arakan a pair of golden fetters with which to bind the Governor-General of India. When warned on one occasion that the British were no mean foe, he said, " I have already defeated the best English soldiers ; give me an army and I will conquer the whole of India."

When the Government of India had definitely decided on war, the wise resolution was come to of pushing the war into the enemy's country. It was very largely a venture into the unknown, as little was known about the people, and even less, apparently, about the climatic conditions. It was sound policy, however, in dealing with an arrogant monarch, to march straight into the heart of his country, instead of confining operations to the border. To have marched an army to Ava, through Arakan, would have been a difficult task, so a force, jointly supplied by Bengal and Madras, was put under the command of Brigadier-General Sir Archibald Campbell. The place of rendezvous was the Andaman Islands, where the troops arrived on 3rd May. Two days later Sir Archibald sailed direct for Rangoon, detaching one part of his force, under Brigadier McNeagh, against the island of Cheduba, and another, under Major Wahab, against the island of Negrais. On the 10th, the fleet anchored in the Rangoon river, and on the following morning sailed up to the town. The Burmese were completely taken by surprise, but a feeble and ill-directed fire was opened upon the ships from a sixteen-gun battery. This was soon silenced and a landing was effected without opposition. Within twenty minutes the British flag was flying in the town, without the loss of a single life, or the discharge of a single musket. It was an absolutely empty town, however, that we had taken, as the inhabitants had all fled. A considerable quantity of ordnance was found, but of very imperfect kind. About the same time the islands of Cheduba and Negrais were taken, after some spirited opposition on the part of the inhabitants of both.

It was thought that the capture of Rangoon, Cheduba and Negrais would bring the Burmese monarch to reason, but there were no signs of this. On the contrary, it was said that his golden-footed Majesty was preparing "to cover the face of the earth with an innumerable host, and to drive back the wild foreigners into the sea." It was by no means an enviable position in which Sir Archibald Campbell found himself. He had Rangoon, certainly, but the rainy season commenced almost immediately after he had taken it, and the rains of Rangoon are so heavy, that it was practically impossible for him to make any further advance until they abated. Harassed by continual incursions of the enemy, threatened with an approaching famine, and reduced by sickness to the greatest debility, the British troops had a weary six months of it. Many attacks were made on stockades which the Burmese erected near Rangoon, but when these were taken the Burmese simply retreated to the jungle and little was gained. An advance up the Irrawaddy was impracticable as no pilot could be procured, and, even if that difficulty could have been surmounted, no land force could accompany the expedition until the rains were over. The only chance of doing anything at once that would further intimidate the Burmese was to secure some of their other maritime possessions. Accordingly, an expedition was sent under Lieutenant-Colonel Miles, who in a few months made himself master of the three seaports, Tavoy, Mergui and Tenasserim.

Colonel Miles had, no doubt, a much better time of it than those who remained in Rangoon, and he was back there in time for the more decisive measures which became possible after the rains were over. The King, finding that the troops he had near Rangoon could not drive the foreigners into the sea, sent down Bundula to undertake the task. His name inspired the Burmese with confidence, and the British troops were delighted at the prospect of at last meeting a less elusive enemy than any they had hitherto encountered. The first encounter took place on 1st December, 1824, and the following extracts from a letter, written by Sir A. Campbell, eight days after the event, will give an idea of what occurred :—" The long-threatened, and, on my part, no less anxiously wished for event, has at length taken place.

BURMESE GIRLS

Photograph by Mr P. Klier, Rangoon

Maha Bandoola, said to be accompanied by the Princes of Tonghoo and Sarrawaddy, appeared in front of my position, on the morning of the 1st instant, at the head of the whole united force of the Burman Empire, amounting, upon the most moderate calculation, to from fifty to sixty thousand men, apparently well-armed, with a numerous artillery, and a body of Cassay horse. Their haughty leader had insolently declared his intention of leading us in captive chains to grace the triumph of the Golden Monarch ; but it has pleased God to expose the vanity of his idle threats, and crown the heroic efforts of my gallant little army with a most complete and signal victory. . . . Early in the morning of the 1st instant, the enemy commenced his operations by a smart attack on our post at Kemmindine, commanded by Major Yates, and garrisoned by the 26th Madras Native Infantry, with a detachment of the Madras European Regiment, supported on the river by as strong a naval force as could be spared. As the day became light it discovered numerous and apparently formidable masses of the advancing enemy issuing from the jungle, and moving at some distance upon both our flanks, for the purpose of surrounding us, which I allowed them to effect without interruption, leaving us only the narrow channel of the Rangoon river unoccupied in our rear. Bandoola had now fully exposed to me his plan of operations, and my own resolution was instantly adopted of allowing, and even encouraging him to bring forth his means and resources from the jungle to the more open country on his left, where I knew I could at any time attend him to advantage."

It is not necessary to repeat the account of the various fights which took place on the 1st and succeeding days between portions of Bundula's army and the British forces. Major Yates, at Kemmendine, had to continue the defence for days, while the naval force there had to resist the assaults of the war-boats, which advanced under cover of tremendous fire-rafts. In the afternoon of the 1st, four hundred men from the 13th Light Infantry, and the 18th Madras Infantry made an attack on the enemy's left, burst through their entrenchments, and returned loaded with arms, standards, and other trophies. It was not, however, until the 5th that the real attack was made on Bundula's left. When that had been dispersed, Sir Archibald Campbell again waited his time to deliver a decisive blow. He says:—"The Burmese left wing thus disposed of, I patiently waited its effect upon the right, posted in so thick a forest as to render any attack in that quarter in a great measure impracticable. On the 6th I had the pleasure of observing that Bandoola had brought up the scattered remnant of his defeated left to strengthen his right and centre, and continued day and night employed in carrying on his approaches in front of the great pagoda. I ordered the artillery to slacken its fire, and the infantry to keep wholly out of sight, allowing him to carry on his fruitless labour with little annoyance or molestation. As I expected, he took system for timidity; and on the morning of the 7th instant, I had his whole force posted in my immediate front—his first line entrenched so close that the soldiers in their barracks could distinctly hear the insolent threats and reproaches of the Burman bravoes.

"The time had now arrived to undeceive them in their sanguine, but ill-founded, hopes. . . . At a quarter before twelve I ordered every gun that would bear on the trenches to open, and their fire was kept up with an effect that never was surpassed; Major Sale at the same time, as directed, making a diversion on the enemy's left and rear. At twelve o'clock the cannonade ceased, and the columns moved forward to their respective points of attack. Every thing was done under my own immediate eye, but, where all behaved so nobly, I cannot particularise ; but I must, in justice, state that Captain Wilson's and Lieutenant-Colonel Parlby's divisions first made an impression, from which the enemy never recovered. They were driven from all their works without a check, abandoning all their guns, with a great quantity of arms of every description ; and certainly not the least amusing part of their formidable preparations was a great number of ladders for escalading the great pagoda, found in rear of their position. The total defeat of Bandoola's army was now most fully accomplished. His loss in killed and wounded, from the nature of the ground, it is impossible to calculate ; but I am confident I do not exceed the fairest limit when I state it at five thousand men. In every other respect the mighty host, which so lately threatened to overwhelm us, now scarcely exists. It commenced its inglorious flight during last night. Humbled, dispersing, and deprived of their arms, they cannot for a length of time again meet us in the field ; and the lesson they have now received will, I am confident, prove a salutary antidote to the native arrogance and vanity of the Burmese nation."

Sir Archibald Campbell, when he penned the last sentence, had yet to learn the character of his foe. He did not understand that the arrogance of the Court could not be brought down until it was itself in danger, and no defeat, however crushing, would intimidate it, so long as that defeat was several hundred miles away from the capital. As to the loss of five thousand men, or of double that number, the King would not greatly concern himself about that. They were his slaves, bound to fight when ordered, and he could still put many thousands into the field. Within a few days Bundula had twenty-five thousand men in a position within three miles of the pagoda, and, as Sir Archibald reports, had "commenced entrenching and stockading with a judgment in point of position such as would do credit to the best instructed engineers of the most civilised and warlike nations." This position, however, was stormed and carried by assault on the 15th December by one thousand three hundred British infantry. It is only fair to add that on this occasion Bundula did not command in person, and the commander to whom he had entrusted the defence of this position was mortally wounded during the assault. On the same day an attack was made upon a fleet of thirty-two Burmese war-boats, of which thirty were captured. The crews had abandoned them, thrown into consternation when they found that the steam-boat "Diana" could move expeditiously even against wind and tide.

Now the position of affairs was greatly altered. Bundula fell back on Donabyu, some distance up the river, and the British found themselves in undisturbed possession of a considerable tract of country outside Rangoon. Transports arrived from India, and the Burmese opened a regular traffic with the British in all articles of consumption. An even more important change just at the moment was that some of the natives volunteered to assist us in the navigation of the river. Our own men, of course, knew nothing of the Irrawaddy, and, without the assistance of native pilots, our progress up that river would have been full of difficulty. On the 13th February, 1825, the start was made. One column, about two thousand strong, went by land, under the command of Sir Archibald Campbell. The other column went by water, under Brigadier-General Cotton, consisting of about one thousand European infantry, with a powerful train of artillery, which was embarked in a flotilla of sixty boats, commanded by Captain Alexander. A smaller force, under Major Sale, was sent to take possession of Bassein, after which it was to join the main body at Donabyu. Brigadier M'Reagh was left in command at Rangoon, and was to employ himself in fortifying that town.

General Cotton, travelling by water, was able to progress more rapidly than the land force, though he encountered more active opposition on the way. On arriving at Donabyu he determined to attack the enemy, who, headed by Bundula, mustered about fifteen thousand, and had fortified their position in the most skilful way. An outer stockade was carried, but the attempt on the second stockade was less successful, so General Cotton had to re-embark his troops and drop down the river four miles to wait for reinforcements Meantime, General Campbell had pushed on towards Prome, not realising the formidable resistance to be encountered at Donabyu. On hearing of the failure to take the second stockade there, he hurried back to General Cotton's assistance. He reached Donabyu on 25th March, and for several days skirmishes of a desultory kind took place, but without much result. On 1st April, a continued fire of rockets was kept up by the British, with little or no return from the enemy. The explanation of this inaction on the part of the Burmese was given next day by one of Bundula's men when the English entered and found the fort almost empty. The man said :—" While he (Bundula) was giving orders to some of his chiefs, the English began throwing bombs, and one of them falling close to the general, burst, and killed him on the spot.

His body was immediately carried away and burnt to ashes. His death was soon known to everyone in the stockade, and the soldiers refused to stay and fight under any other commander. The chiefs lost all influence over their men, every individual thinking only of providing for his own personal safety."

The loss of Bundula was a very serious loss indeed to the Burmese. He was a stern disciplinarian, and kept together the raw levies which constituted his army in a way no one else could do. In many ways, too, he showed marked skill as a general. The position and defences at Donabyu elicited the admiration of his opponents, who said that, as a field work, they would have done credit to the most scientific engineer. Though during the fighting near Rangoon he was never under fire, he did not hesitate to show courage when necessary. At Donabyu he declared that he would conquer or die, and set his men an example of the courage he required from all. Against any Asiatic foe he would have been invincible; but the system, the discipline, the organisation and the arms of the British were too much for him. One anecdote related of him is that in the early part of the operations he expressed a desire to see one of the shells, which were working such havoc among his men. One was found, which, though it was still fizzing dreadfully, the Burmese thought must be a failure, so they took it to show to Bundula. Before it actually reached him, it burst, killing its bearers and everyone near it. Bundula was thunderstruck, and for the whole of that day it is said that his courage failed him.

After the taking of Donabyu the British pushed on to Prome, but were met by messengers from the authorities of that town intimating the willingness of the Government to conclude a peace. Suspecting that this was merely a device to gain time, Sir Archibald replied that after he had taken Prome he would be ready to listen to any overtures. On arrival it was found that active preparations were being made for a vigorous defence, but as the British arrived before their fortifications were completed, the Burmese troops retired at night, and on 25th April, General Campbell entered the town without firing a shot. As another rainy season was now about to set in, which the British probably expected to be as severe at Prome as in Rangoon, it was decided to fix our head-quarters at Prome. Toungoo was also taken, so that all the country from Prome and Toungoo down to the sea-coast was practically under British control. The people returned to the towns and villages, and carried on their usual avocations under a temporary system of control established by the invaders, the Burmese officials having fled.

During the rains of 1825, while the British were quietly administering the territory they held, the Court of Ava was organising an army of seventy thousand men to overwhelm the small British force. A letter was sent in October by Sir Archibald Campbell to the Burmese head-quarters urging on the chiefs the propriety of coming to terms. This led to a meeting between commissioners from both sides, but no agreement could be reached. After the conference, the Burmese army marched to the gates of Prome, its general having previously sent the following laconic epistle to the British commander :—" If you wish for peace, you may go away ; but if you ask either money or territory, no friendship can exist between us. This is Burman custom."

To oppose the formidable force now gathering around Prome, General Campbell had five thousand men, of whom only three thousand were British. As the

Burmese plan this time was to establish a blockade, it was necessary to frustrate this scheme, so, on 1st December, our marine and land forces advanced, and, after a fight of some hours, succeeded in driving the Burmese back to a stockade they had erected some miles distant, on the heights of Napadi. It would have been folly to let them remain there, but it took four days' hard fighting to drive them from this position. On the 5th December, however, victory was complete, and the Burmese army was again reduced to a vast host of fugitives, dispersed in all directions. It was now determined to advance at once to Ava, and on 9th December the start was made. On the 29th, when the British army reached Malwun, a Commissioner arrived from Ava with power to conclude a treaty. On 1st January, 1826, an agreement was made, fifteen days being allowed for its ratification by the King. At the end of that time, a further period of delay was asked for, but Sir Archibald's reply was that if the Burmese troops evacuated Malwun at once, he would wait some days longer; if not, he would attack Malwun without delay. The Burmese refused to evacuate Malwun, so, on 19th January, they were attacked and driven out. In the house of a half-brother of the King, who was in command, was found a sum of about forty thousand rupees, and both the English and Burmese copies of the treaty, signed and sealed as they had been at the meeting. It was evident that the treaty had never been sent to the King at all, and that the delays for his ratification of it were merely a device to gain time. Sir Archibald sent the treaty to the Burmese Commissioner with a polite note saying that he had doubtless left it behind in the hurry of his departure from Malwun, and would, perhaps, now consider it a more acceptable document than he had previously. The Commissioner politely thanked Sir Archibald for returning the treaty, and added that the Burmese had also left behind a large sum of money, which, doubtless, the British general would also return.

The British army now resumed its march on Ava. On 31st January, it was met by Dr Price, an American missionary, and an Englishman named Sandford, an assistant-surgeon, who had been taken prisoner some months before. These gentlemen had been sent on parole to ascertain the lowest terms on which peace could be secured. The same terms which had been offered at Malwun were repeated. These were the cession of Arakan and of Cachar, and the payment by the Burmese of a crore of rupees. The delegates then returned to Ava, General Campbell promising that for twelve days to come he would not advance beyond Pagan. Meantime, the King had resolved on making another stand, so a fresh army was despatched to Pagan. After defeating this, General Campbell resumed his march on Ava. Forty-five miles from that city, at a place called Yandabu, he was met by Dr Price and Mr Sandford, accompanied by two ministers of state and all the British prisoners who had been taken during the war. The prisoners, both Europeans and sepoys, presented a sorry spectacle. They were clothed in filthy rags; they were worn to skin and bone; and their haggard countenances, and sunken, wandering eyes told too plainly the story of their long suffering. The two ministers brought with them twenty-five lakhs of rupees as the first instalment of the money payment demanded; and they brought also an authority to accept such terms of peace as the British general might demand.

The treaty of Yandabu was signed on 24th February, 1826. By it, the King undertook to abstain from any future interference in Assam, Cachar and Jyntea. He ceded the province of Arakan, the Yomadaung mountains to form the boundary line between British and Burmese territory. He ceded, also, the conquered provinces of Ye, Tavoy, Mergui and Tenasserim, the Salween river to be the boundary between British and Burmese territory. He further agreed to pay an indemnity of one crore of rupees in four instalments. On payment of the first instalment, the British would retire to Rangoon; on payment of the second, they would leave the King's dominions, leaving the remaining fifty lakhs to be paid during the following two years.

It is a little difficult to understand why the British insisted on taking over Tenasserim. It is true that they had taken various ports on the Tenasserim coast, but so had they taken Rangoon and the country behind it, all of which they evacuated. The war had been undertaken in defence of Bengal, so the annexation of Arakan, Assam, Cachar and Jyntea is intelligible enough. That served to cut Burma off from India, and in the Yomadaung mountains we got a much better boundary line between us and a troublesome neighbour, than the river Naf had been. Moreover, Arakan, Assam, Cachar and Jyntea adjoin India, so the administration and defence of these could be arranged with comparative ease. But in taking over Tenasserim, we took over a province isolated from the rest of our Indian possessions. We could only reach it by sea, a very great disadvantage in days when sailing vessels were still the chief means of communication. It gave us the Burmese again as neighbours at a fresh point, and with only a river, the Salween, as the boundary between us and them. Finally, it gave us the Siamese as neighbours, and though in the treaty with Burma the King of Siam is described as our "good and faithful ally," it seems somewhat rash to have brought ourselves into such close contact with him, as the long land frontier between Tenasserim and Siam involved. Certainly, the Siamese and the Burmese were hereditary enemies of each other, but the possession of Tenasserim involved the risk of our being drawn into their quarrels, a risk which might have been avoided had we not annexed Tenasserim. No harm came of it, but it might easily have led to serious complications in Indo-China at a time when the consolidation of our Indian empire was still far from complete.

As to the Burmese, the following is the account of the war as recorded in their chronicle :—" In the years 1186 and 1187, the white strangers from the west fastened a quarrel upon the Lord of the Golden Palace. They landed at Rangoon, took that place and Prome, and were permitted to advance as far as Yandabu ; for the King, from motives of piety and regard for life, made no preparation whatever to oppose them. The strangers had spent vast sums of money in their enterprise, so that by the time they reached Yandabu their resources were exhausted, and they were in great distress. They then petitioned the King, who, in his clemency and generosity, sent them large sums of money to pay their expenses back, and ordered them out of the country."

CHAPTER XI.

A.D. 1826 TO 1853

IN January, 1827, the Talaings, headed by Maung Tsat, the Governor of Syriam, made an effort to throw off the Burmese yoke. Joined by the Karens, they surrounded Rangoon, but were defeated, and a number of them took refuge in Tenasserim, which was now British territory.

In April, 1830, Major Burney arrived at Ava as the first English Resident. At first his presence was resented by the Burmese King, and the ministers urged that an embassy once in ten years, similar to the arrangement with China, would be more suitable. But the British Resident gradually gained some influence, and made some progress towards a better understanding. He was able to urge successfully Burma's claim to the Kubo valley; Burmese envoys were sent to India and, for the first time, the King of Burma wrote a letter to the Governor-General.

Ever since the treaty of Yandabu, King Bagyidaw had felt much humiliated. He became subject to fits of melancholy, and by 1831, he had become insane. His brother, the Prince of Tharrawaddy, presided over a commission of regency, but the influence of the chief queen and her brother was predominant, and Tharrawaddy found it expedient to absent himself. He remained in seclusion for six years, during which he made preparations for the struggle which he saw must come. In 1837, he found he must fight for his own safety; raised the standard of revolt and succeeded in securing the crown. The deposed King lived as a prisoner, but well treated, for eight years.

King Tharrawaddy, before his accession to the throne, had treated the British Resident, Major Burney, with courtesy and considerable deference, but after his accession he took a very different stand on this point. He refused to hold any direct communication with anyone but the English Sovereign in person. The Governor-General of India was only a servant, and, consequently, should correspond with the Governor of Rangoon, not with the King of Burma. As to the treaty of Yandabu, it had been made with his predecessor, and Tharrawaddy declined to be bound by the acts of another. He was willing to treat Major Burney as a private gentleman, but would not recognise him as the representative of the Governor-General, and any allusion to the treaty of Yandabu would incur the royal displeasure. Under these circumstances, Major Burney's residence in the capital could be of no advantage in any way, so the mission was withdrawn. Kyaukmyaung had been made the capital, but, after a few months, it was moved to Amarapura, which had been the capital of Bodopra, King Tharrawaddy's grandfather.

King Bagyidaw was still alive and under restraint, the queen and her brother, who had practically driven Tharrawaddy from his position on the council of regency, were in close imprisonment; but there were others of the royal blood who might raise a rebellion with some prospect of success. These were all either murdered or driven into exile by orders of the King. Thinking himself now safe, he abandoned himself to a life of low pleasures. He became a slave to drink, and in moments of fury he would indulge in horrible cruelties. On one occasion he amused himself by trying his new rifle on some innocent men ; and on another, he scored a chess-board with his sword on the back of an unfortunate man who was made to bow down for the purpose. Practically he was now as mad as the brother whom he had deposed, and now kept under guard. An unsuccessful revolt was punished by forty men, women and children being shut up in a bamboo house and burnt to death.

In 1838, Colonel Benson was deputed from India as Resident, in place of Major Burney, who had given up the attempt to establish friendly relations as quite hopeless. He brought valuable presents for the King, but was treated with studied discourtesy throughout his journey. At Prome he was advised not to proceed further. When he came within sight of the capital, his vessel grounded on a sand bank. All communication with the town had been stopped ; and the only message he received was that the King would receive him as a private individual only, and that His Majesty repudiated the treaty of Yandabu. Colonel Benson thereupon returned to Rangoon, leaving his assistant, Captain McLeod who was younger and more sanguine, to see what he could do. Captain McLeod was not easily discouraged, but when month after month passed, leaving him still on his sandbank, he, too, at last, gave up the attempt as hopeless and returned to Rangoon in 1840. This ended all attempts at diplomatic intercourse with the Burmese King. The overweening pride of almost every member of the Alompra dynasty foredoomed to failure almost every attempt in this direction, and it is surprising that the Government of India should have persisted in these attempts in spite of so many failures. With King Tharrawaddy they were specially hopeless, as by this time he was merely a drunken and insane savage.

A confederacy of the Shan States next made a bid for independence, but it was unsuccessful, and, as the ex-queen of Bagyidaw and her brother were supposed to have instigated it from their prison, they had to pay the penalty. The queen was crushed to death by elephants, and her brother, with others supposed to be implicated, met equally cruel deaths. In 1841, Tharrawaddy came to Rangoon, with an idea of doing something for the recovery of Arakan and Tenasserim, but, in spite of all his bombastic pride, he thought better of that, and did nothing beyond ordering festivities on a large scale. On his return to his capital, the symptoms of insanity became more marked, and in 1845, his son, the Prome Prince, kept him under restraint. Then there was a partial recovery, during which the Prome Prince thought it better for his own safety to seek refuge in the Shan States. The recovery proved very temporary, however, and then another son, the Tarukmaw Prince, took him in charge, and kept a guard over him until his death in 1846.

King Tharrawaddy was succeeded by his son, the Prince of Pagan, who ruled, or at least occupied the throne, under the name Pagan Min. One of his first acts was to order the deaths of his brother, the Tarukmaw Prince, and all his family. Pagan Min then abandoned himself to pleasure, leaving the control of affairs to his ministers, who were unscrupulous men for the most part. So long as the governors of the different parts of the country sent in money in sufficient quantity to the treasury, they could do what they liked. This must have led to oppression of the people everywhere, but it was no very great departure from the usual custom, and, so far as the Burmese were concerned, it might have gone on for some time without any very serious consequences.

In time, of course, the governors would have aimed at complete independence, and a disintegrating process would have set in, until someone of a very different mettle from Pagan Min managed to seize the supreme power.

The Governor of Rangoon, however, one Maung Ôk, had not only the King's subjects to deal with, but a considerable number of foreigners as well, Europeans Armenians, Portuguese, and natives of India, who had settled in Rangoon to trade. The neighbouring port, Maulmain, was thriving under British rule, and the Europeans there were pushing and energetic people, who did a considerable trade, chiefly in timber, and, for some years, did a fair amount of ship-building as well. A newspaper, the *Maulmain Chronicle*, had been started in 1837, and the numbers of that paper still extant give a vivid impression of what life in Maulmain was in those days. The European community was very small, and it was very much isolated from the rest of India, but the people were very tenacious of their rights, always ready to protest vigorously whenever they thought themselves wronged by the local officials or by the Government of India. They regarded themselves as "colonists," and many of them made Maulmain their permanent home. With their compatriots in Maulmain enjoying freedom of this kind, and prospering under British rule, the Europeans whose business required them to reside in Rangoon were not likely to be very patient under the tyranny of Maung Ok, the Burmese governor. One of them, Mr Crisp, ventured on a criticism of the Burmese Government in a letter to a Calcutta paper. He meant the letter to be published anonymously, but unfortunately, the editor published the writer's name. A copy of this paper was sent to the Burmese authorities, and Mr Crisp being in

Maulmain at the time, his son was arrested, and detained as hostage until Mr Crisp returned to Rangoon. This he did as soon as he could, in order to get his son released. By that time, apparently, Maung Ôk's indignation had cooled, or he persuaded himself that it did not matter what foreigners thought of Burmese rule, so he contented himself with banishing Mr Crisp from Burmese territory.

While the barque, *Monarch*, was coming up the Rangoon river, the vessel grounded, and, to escape blame, the Burmese pilot jumped overboard and was drowned. Captain Shepherd, the commander, was summoned before Maung Ôk, and condemned to imprisonment for the murder of a Burmese subject. Later on, he was charged with embezzlement, and, though acquitted, was made to pay a fine of five hundred rupees. Several of the crew, also, were maltreated, confined, and only liberated on payment of money.

Captain Lewis, the commander of the *Champion*, was also seized in Rangoon, and charged with the murder of one of his crew—a native who had died at sea. For this he had to pay a fine of two hundred and fifty rupees, the governor showing him irons and threatening to send him in these irons to Amarapura. On one pretext or another Captain Lewis had to pay the better part of a thousand rupees altogether, before he could get away from Rangoon.

Major Bogle, the Commissioner of Tenasserim, represented to the Government of India the unjust treatment being meted out to British subjects by the governor of Rangoon; whereupon a remonstrance was sent, and a demand made for an indemnity of ten thousand rupees for the losses incurred by Captains Shepherd and Lewis. At the same time Commodore Lambert was despatched from Calcutta in the *Fox*, accompanied by the war-steamer, *Tenasserim*. He arrived in Rangoon on 25th November, 1851, and arranged that a deputation of officers should wait on the governor two days later to endeavour to settle matters amicably. On the morning of the 27th, however, further acts of oppression of British subjects came to the knowledge of Commodore Lambert, so he withdrew the original demands, and sent a letter to the governor, saying that matters must remain in abeyance until he received further instructions from India. Maung Ôk promptly issued an order forbidding, under pain of death, any of the foreign residents of Rangoon to communicate with Commodore Lambert. He also armed a vessel in the river and kept an army of ten thousand men in readiness.

Before leaving Calcutta, Commodore Lambert had received a letter from Lord Dalhousie to Pagan Min, which was to be forwarded if matters could not be settled with the governor of Rangoon. In this letter, the removal of the tyrannical governor was required, as well as the payment of the indemnity. This letter had been forwarded as soon as it was apparent that nothing could be done with Maung Ôk, and on 1st January, 1852, the King's reply was sent on board the *Fox*, the letter being conveyed with every possible form of Burmese pomp, white elephants, golden umbrellas, and streets lined with saluting soldiers; all, of course, in honour of the royal letter, not in the least intended to reflect any glory on its recipients. The letter expressed friendly sentiments and said the governor would be superseded by a high officer whom the King had sent to adjust the difficulties that had arisen. This high officer, Maung Mhôn, the new governor, arrived on 3rd January, but no intimation was sent to Commodore Lambert. From other sources the Commodore learned that the old governor had left with every mark of respect, carrying away a large sum of money, and that one of the first acts of the new governor had been to repeat Maung Ôk's threat of death to anyone daring to communicate with the British vessels. On 5th January, the deputy governor of Dalla came on board to intimate that the new governor was ready to receive a deputation with a view to an amicable settlement. When the officers presented themselves, however, the next day, they were treated with disrespect and insult ; they were told that the Viceroy was asleep, and no one would even receive the Commodore's letter. The tactics were thoroughly Burmese, the object being to impress on everyone that Maung Mhôn, as the Viceroy of the King, was a very great person indeed, while the British officers were of no importance whatsoever, and must await the Viceroy's pleasure. Had this treatment being tamely submitted to and another interview sought, it could only have led to a repetition of the same tactics, probably with even more open insults and disrespect.

It is difficult for anyone who has not had personal experience of it to understand the way in which the Burmese regarded such things, and the infinite pains they would take to humiliate anyone seeking an interview with the King or any exalted official. They had really brought it to a fine art. The following episode in the writer's own experience will probably make the thing more intelligible. Towards the end of 1870, the merchants of Rangoon determined to send up a consignment of goods to Bhamo, to test by practical experiment whether anything could be done from there to increase the trade with Western China. It was a joint venture, and, to my great delight, I was selected to go in charge of it, though I had been only a few months out, and was only twenty-three years of age. My instructions were to rent an office in Bhamo and sell the goods for export to Western China. On the way up by steamer I had to remain for several days in Mandalay, and there, on one pretext or another, I was called to the Palace almost every day. When I returned, after three months at Bhamo, the same thing was repeated with even greater insistence, not a single day passing without my getting a summons to the Palace. The knotty point discussed at all these interviews was whether the goods I had sold in Bhamo were liable to one per cent. transit duty only, or to five per cent. import duty. I claimed the former; the ministers insisted that the latter was due, as the goods had been *sold* in Burma, though they were to be exported. Eventually I found that according to the English version of the treaty I was right, and according to the Burmese version they were right, so I announced my intention of going by the next steamer to Rangoon, and leaving the British Resident and the Burmese officials to settle which version of the treaty was to hold good. The minister, to whom I announced this, insisted I must see the King again before leaving, and must come the following day for that purpose. I objected, on the ground that I had seen nothing of Mandalay during my stay, and wanted the following day, which would be my last, to go to Mandalay hill. I offered to see the King at once if he would see me then, or to leave the usual parting gift with the minister to hand over with the usual civil speeches. All I could get was an assurance that if I came to the palace at ten the following morning the King would see me at once, and that I would have the whole day from about eleven o'clock free to see Mandalay. Trusting to this promise, I was at the palace promptly at ten the next morning. The minister met me, saying:

"I am just going to see the King, and will send for you directly." An hour or two later, he returned, saying the King could not see me then, and that I must return the next day. This I absolutely refused to do, so the minister again went away, saying he was going to see the King again, and would send for me. By the time he returned I was very hungry and was just leaving to go back to the Residency in quest of lunch, so he handed over his own mid-day meal to me. It consisted of fruit only, and was not very satisfying, but I was glad to get it, being quite determined either to get the interview with the King over that day, or to have it dispensed with altogether. All the afternoon, messengers were kept plying between the King and the minister as to my interview; every injunction that I should go the next day being met by a firm but civil refusal on the ground that I had to leave for Rangoon that day. At last, towards six o'clock in the evening came an order that my interpreter and I were to be taken to the women's apartments, where the King was. It should have been regarded as a great honour, but I was too exasperated and too hungry to feel that, finding instead some satisfaction at the sight of the King's dinner getting cold during our interview. His Majesty was very gracious, offering to make me a rich man if I would stay in Upper Burma. The whole episode is trivial enough, but when one realises that so much trouble could be taken to keep a young mercantile assistant dancing attendance at the palace, not from any personal dislike, but merely on principle, apparently, and that in the time of King Mindôn, one of the best of the Alompra line, it is easier to understand that Maung Mhôn was merely playing the same game when Commodore Lambert's officers were told he was asleep.

Commodore Lambert, as representative of the Viceroy of India, claiming fair treatment for British subjects residing in Burma, had to prove in some way that he had not come to Rangoon to be trifled with. He accordingly seized the Burmese war-ship and dropped a little way down the river. As the royal ship was being towed down the river by the *Hermes*, a fire was opened on the *Fox* from the shore, but this was soon silenced, while the batteries on the opposite side of the river, from which a fire was directed on the *Hermes*, were soon reduced to silence by the heavy guns of that vessel. Next day the deputy governor of Dalla came on board, to try and secure the return of the captured vessel, but was told that no further negociations would be listened to until Maung Mhôn apologised in person. This, of course, he was not in the least likely to do. Indeed it is very doubtful whether the poor governor of Dalla would dare to deliver such a message to his superior. Commodore Lambert then went to Calcutta, having first arranged for the safety of the British residents by sending them to Maulmain. The following account of their exodus from Rangoon is evidently from the pen of an eye-witness :—" The *Proserpine* steamer ran close into the main wharf, and eight or ten of the boats from the frigate and steamers came to the shore to protect and receive the fugitives. Meanwhile the streets were filled with armed Burmese, and Burmese officers were moving to and fro on horseback, threatening all who gave assistance to the foreigners ; in consequence of which not a coolie could be procured. All classes of foreigners—Moguls, Mussulmans, Armenians, Portuguese, and English—were seen crowding down to the river with boxes and bundles, and whatever they could carry, but they were obliged, generally to abandon all the property they possessed. Mr

Kincaid, the American missionary, left his library, consisting of more than a thousand volumes, the collection of twenty years, behind him to be destroyed, too happy, however, to find his wife and children safe under the British flag." There were nearly four hundred refugees in all, thus dumped into Maulmain, and as many of them had been compelled to abandon all their property, the hospitality of Maulmain must have been somewhat heavily taxed.

The result of Commodore Lambert's visit to Calcutta was a further remonstrance from the Government of India to that of Burma, but this produced only an evasive reply. To this a reply was sent to the effect that, unless the demands for an apology from the Governor of Rangoon for his insults to the British officers, and for an indemnity for the wrongs inflicted on British subjects were complied with before the 1st of April, immediate war would result. It was thought that this would suffice to bring Pagan Min to his knees, but, in this instance again, we reckoned without any proper understanding of Burmese ignorance of the outer world, and of their stupendous pride. Pagan Min, moreover, had been led to believe that the war of 1826 had so weakened the power of the Indian Government that a further war would have little chance of success, even if it were ventured on at all. He did send an answer to the ultimatum, but it was merely to the effect that it was his servants, not himself, who were insolent, and that he desired to be communicated with in future through Major Bogle, the Commissioner of Tenasserim, and not through Commodore Lambert. In March, some Burmese arrived in Calcutta, and reported that twenty thousand men were ready to stand against us, and to dispute every inch of the way from Rangoon to the capital.

The British provinces of Arakan and Tenasserim might well have been a source of danger at this crisis, had there been any disaffection there. But neither the Talaings of Tenasserim, nor the Arakanese, had any love for the Burmese, whose former oppressions were not forgotten. The people had learnt to appreciate British rule, and had no wish to return to the old order of things. Still there was some danger of Burmese troops invading these provinces, and, in the case of Arakan, at least, news was received of such an invasion being contemplated. The *Precursor*, a very magnificent steamer of the P.O.S. Navigation Company, was despatched from Calcutta to Arakan, with half a company of native artillery. When she arrived at Kyaukpyu, the native boats fled, as the boatmen had never seen a vessel of that size; but there was no enemy in the field. Had there been an invasion, the Burmese army would probably have marched through the Aeng Pass, so an officer was sent there, but instead of troops he found only peaceful traders, and trade going on as if nothing had happened, or was likely to happen. The Irrawaddy is so completely the highway of Burma, that it is very largely along its valley that the question of empire has been decided. Those living in the more remote parts of the country were so isolated, in the complete absence of roads and railways, that they lived more or less unmolested, and pursued their usual avocations throughout the wars. Some of the men may have been drawn into the armies of the combatants, and local disputes between petty local chiefs may have resulted in small local wars at times, but the chief burden of all the great wars must have fallen mainly from the earliest times on those who lived in the Irrawaddy valley. In the more mountainous parts of the country, well removed from the great natural highway of the river, numerous tribes have lived in such complete seclusion for many centuries that they have evolved distinctive languages and customs, have not even been absorbed into the Buddhist religion, and have never had any share whatever in the main current of the national life.

The first Burmese war had given us some knowledge of the country, and had taught us especially that it was well to push through any military operations before the rains commenced. But as the King of Burma had been given till 1st April to come to terms, this only left some six weeks or two months before the heavy rain would begin. General Godwin was selected to command the expedition, as he had already fought in Burma and knew something of the country. He had 5,800 soldiers under his immediate command, and about 2,500 sailors and marines under Commodore Lambert. It was decided to commence operations by taking Martaban, opposite Maulmain, but in Burmese territory, the river Salween being then the boundary between British and Burmese territory. The Burmese considered Martaban a position of great importance, and the place is one in which a very formidable defence might be made. The General and Admiral Austen commanding in the Eastern seas, who had come from Penang to join the expedition, reached Maulmain on 4th April, and the following day the war-steamers opened fire on Martaban. A storming party, under Colonel Reignolds, then took the town, with only one wing of the Royal Irish. After making the necessary arrangements for the protection of the place, the General and Admiral hurried back to Rangoon, but before narrating their doings there it will be well to finish with Martaban. The Burmese governor thought he could retake the place after the bulk of the British troops had gone.

Pagan Min had sent Shwe Lôn, a notorious dacoit, to assist in this enterprise, the loss of his head to be the penalty of failure. The 26th April was fixed as a lucky day for the attack, so the attempt was made on that day. The attack was a bold one, but was as boldly responded to, and when the report of the artillery was heard in Maulmain, the *Feroze* was able to join in at once from her position opposite the office of Messrs Graceman & Co., though that was two or three miles away from the position occupied by the Burmese. Reinforcements were also sent at once from the Maulmain cantonment to the assistance of the small garrison in Martaban. The result was that the attack failed completely, and the Burmese fled in confusion.

Meanwhile General Godwin and Admiral Austen had arrived in Rangoon, and on Easter Sunday, the 11th of April, the attack commenced. The *Sesostris, Mozaffer* and *Feroze* destroyed the well fortified stockade on the Dalla side of the river, and enabled the 18th Royal Irish, with a body of marines, to land and drive away the enemy. The *Serpent* and *Phlegethon* took up their position opposite Kemendine, and the *Fox* poured her broadsides on the defences on the Rangoon side of the river, eventually striking a powder magazine, the explosion of which reduced the stockade in which it was situated, an extensive and well-fortified one, to ashes. Early in the morning of the 12th, a part of the artillery as well as the 15th Light Infantry, the 18th Royal Irish, and the 40th Bengal Native Infantry, landed without opposition, but had not gone far before the Burmese artillery opened fire on them. Before the pagoda could be attacked it was necessary to take a stockade on the east of the Pagoda Hill, known as the White House Stockade. This was carried, but not without severe loss. It was evident that the Burmese had profited by the lessons of 1825, and were now a more skilful foe than they had been then. There were twenty-five pieces of cannon, some of them eighteen-pounders, on the upper terrace of the Shwe Dagon pagoda, and heavy guns were mounted in other parts of the town. There was some difficulty in landing the heavy battery guns, but by the 14th, General Godwin found himself ready to attack the pagoda. It was stubbornly defended, but eventually it was carried after hard fighting and considerable loss on both sides. The possession of the pagoda carried with it the command of the town. General Godwin's next care was to capture the town of Bassein, which commanding, as it does, a large branch of the Irrawaddy, is a place of strategic importance. This town he took on the 19th May; left a garrison of five hundred men, and returned to Rangoon in time to celebrate Queen Victoria's birthday there on the 24th.

Meantime the Talaings had seized the opportunity of the defeat of the Burmese at Rangoon to take their old capital, Pegu, from the Burmese. After the first Burmese war many Talaings had emigrated to Tenasserim to escape Burmese oppression, and numbers of Burmans had also gone to secure a more just rule than that of their own kings. Probably a great many more of both would have gone had it not been for the difficulty of getting their families away. Under the Burmese kings, when a man left his native place, his wife and children were supposed to remain as hostages for his return. Obscure individuals might sometimes evade this law, especially if they lived near the frontier, but for the more prominent people anywhere, it was very difficult to evade it; and if a long journey had to be taken to reach the frontier, it was almost impossible for any family to escape. The Talaings had, no doubt, been severely oppressed by the Burmese after the British withdrew from Rangoon, and their sympathies were now entirely on the British side. But if the British were again to retire they knew that, whatever promise to the contrary might be exacted from the Burmese King, a heavy vengeance would fall on them for any open help they might have given during the war. General Godwin thoroughly understood their position and he had so much confidence in the Talaings that he said, after the fall of Rangoon, that "if he had the authority to promise annexation, he would levy a militia of these fellows, and go with them and a portion of our force, to Prome at once." He was not authorised, however, to promise annexation, but when the Talaing insurrection against the Burmese began, and had been to some extent successful, he sent a small body of British soldiers and sepoys to help them to take Pegu. After it was taken, it was handed over to the Talaings, as the British army in Burma was not sufficiently numerous to allow of garrisons being left in any places but those of real strategic importance.

Early in June, Captain Brooking took the *Proserpine* up the river, and succeeded in getting within thirty miles of Prome. The following month a more formidable expedition was sent to Prome, passing on its way a force of seven thousand men under Maung Gyi, a son of the great Bundula who had lost his life at Donabyu in the former war. Prome was undefended, the governor having fled, and the British force took possession without opposition. It was decided, however, that it was not advisable to leave any small garrison in charge of Prome, as the decisive battle of the campaign was likely to be fought there. The iron cannon found in Prome were disabled, and thrown into the river, while three brass guns and a mortar were carried away. After an occupation of twenty-four hours only, the British force evacuated Prome to return to Rangoon, there to await the reinforcements necessary to end the struggle. On the way down an engagement took place in which the Burmese lost five brass guns on field carriages, and some war-boats with a large quantity of arms and ammunition.

Lord Dalhousie visited Rangoon towards the end of July and satisfied himself that everything was going on well. As the rains were now on in full force, and the reinforcements from India had not arrived, there was nothing to be done but wait. By the end of September, however, another advance on Prome was made, and that town was reached on 9th October. After a short engagement, in which only one man was killed and twelve wounded on the British side, the Burmese abandoned the town. Maung Gyi held a strongly fortified position near Yathemyo, and had 18,000 men under his command, but he was conspicuously lacking in the qualities that had distinguished his father Bundula, and, three days after the capture of Prome, he surrendered to the British, while his soldiers fled in all directions.

Meantime the Talaings had not been able to hold Pegu. The Burmese garrison from Martaban had to live as best they could after the fall of that town, and hearing that the Talaings had possession of Pegu, a number of these marauders combined and took it. General Godwin could send no assistance to the Talaings until he had settled the business of Prome, where he had every reason to expect a much more formidable resistance than was actually made. Immediately after the fall of Prome, General Godwin turned his attention to Pegu, but it was the 20th of November before the expedition reached Pegu. Meantime the Burmese had strongly fortified the position, but the following day the British were in possession, and on the 23rd, a number of Talaings came in. A garrison of 300 men of the Madras Fusiliers and 200 of the 5th M.N.I., was left in Pegu, under the command of Major Hill. It was far too small a garrison under the circumstances, as the marauding soldiery from Martaban proved a much more formidable foe than the army under Bundula's degenerate son had been. Major Hill, with his five hundred Sepoys and his untrained Talaings, was soon hemmed in by eight thousand Burmese. More ammunition and a body of 240 Fusiliers were sent to his relief, but they were unable to communicate with Major Hill, and returned to Rangoon. General Godwin then set out at once with twelve hundred men, in two steamers and several boats, while Captain Strut, with a land column, was despatched to drive off the Burmese who were likely to give trouble on the right bank of the river. The relief of the small garrison in Pegu was effected on 14th December, but it had been very hard pressed for some time, and Major Hill well deserved the praise which Lord Dalhousie expressed to him six months later, when offering him the command of the Gwalior contingent, adding :—" And I beg you to regard the act as being at once a testimony of your distinguished personal merit, and a compliment to the gallant force you led so well, and a mark of respect to the army of the Presidency to which you belong."

The relief of Pegu practically ended the second Burmese war, though there was some subsequent fighting with dacoit bands before the country was entirely subdued. No treaty was signed, but in January, 1853, the annexation of the province of Pegu was formally declared by the Government of India. The frontier line had been demarcated by Major Allan, from whom the village of Alanmyo gets its name. Meantime civil war had broken out in Upper Burma, the party of revolt against Pagan Min being headed by his half-brother Mindôn Min. On the 18th of February, 1853, the latter made himself master of the capital and of the palace, the deposed Pagan Min being allowed to live in confinement, while Mindôn Min reigned in his stead. By the end of June, though the new King would sign no treaty, the British Government was satisfied with his expressions of good-will, withdrew the river blockade, relaxed the military preparations, and issued a declaration of peace.

CHAPTER XII.

A.D. 1853 TO 1885

IN his "Alaungpra Dynasty," Gray says:—"Of all the descendants of Alaungpra, Mindôn Min alone shone out with those qualities which befit the ruler of a large kingdom." Though Mindôn was, in some ways, the best of the lot, he scarcely deserves the high praise Gray gives him. He was free from the cruelty and ferocity which had marked several of his predecessors, culminating in madness in more than one instance. He was religious and well-intentioned, no doubt, and was anxious to secure peace for his country He lived on better terms with the British than any of his predecessors had done; but he could not have failed to realise, as they did, that resistance was useless. He was a boy of twelve when Arakan and Tenasserim were annexed, and just as he came to the throne, Pegu was annexed also. He had the sense to accept the inevitable, and to do so with a fairly good grace. But of the qualities which befit a great ruler there is little trace. Some reforms in the administration he tried to introduce, but with so little success that during his reign numbers of his people continued to migrate to British territory to escape the tyranny of Mindôn's officials. But for the difficulty of getting a man's family away, the exodus from independent to British Burma would have been greater than it was. It scarcely shows great administrative qualities in a ruler when such precautions have to be enforced to check emigration. Of soldierly qualities he had none. The army degenerated so much in the interval between the second and third Burmese wars that the resistance in the latter was absolutely insignificant. Yet Europeans had been appointed to military offices; but an efficient army cannot be created and maintained without considerable and steady expenditure of money, and that Mindôn would not supply. The courtly and charming Frenchman, General de Facieu, who was at the head of the Burmese army in 1870, and for some years both before and after that date, had a manifestly hopeless task. The talents of a Napoleon would not have sufficed to create and keep an efficient army under such conditions as he had to face.

Mindôn's mind was chiefly taken up with trade, but he knew nothing of political economy, and did not understand that, without security for life and property, without roads or railways, and without moderate and settled dues, trade cannot expand. Nature had given the magnificent highway of the Irrawaddy, but away from that and other navigable streams, the only means of transport was by mules and oxen, or by porters, all obliged to make their way as best they could without roads or bridges. In addition to this, every petty chieftain and every official through whose territory a trade caravan passed, levied blackmail on the unfortunate traders. This in itself, would have been enough to strangle trade, but matters were made worse by King Mindôn's own interferences in the shape of royal monopolies, and in other ways. Possibly he might have been a fairly successful merchant, as far as that was possible under such conditions, had he not been the King, but the mixing of trade and of government was fatal to both. His merit was that he was comparatively rational and sane, good hearted and well-intentioned, which is more than can be said for most of his house. Even his pride was more moderate than that of most of his predecessors, though it was not wholly lacking. I have already given an instance of the way it worked out in the petty humiliations inflicted on anyone who had occasion to visit the palace. At that time, on my journey from Mandalay to Bhamo, there was on board the steamer a Burmese official who had spent eight years in Paris. This man remarked to me one day that the King really believed that Mandalay was a far finer city than London or Paris. When I asked why neither he nor any of the other officials who had visited Europe, put the King right on this point, he laughed, and said that any one bold enough to speak the truth on such a point would soon pay for his temerity with his life. Either he or one of the other passengers, chiefly Europeans who knew Upper Burma well, then told the following story of a well meant attempt at such enlightenment of the King. His Majesty had expressed a desire to see a map of the world. When it was brought he asked to have England pointed out to him. This was done, and he at once said :—" Yes, I always knew that England is a very small country." Then he asked to have Burma pointed out, but when this was done correctly he got so angry at its being so small that the unfortunate man who was giving this lesson in geography hastened to cover as much of the map as he could with both hands and to say that was Burma. As it was about half the world, the King was then quite satisfied.

In 1854, Mindôn Min sent an embassy to Calcutta to negotiate for the restoration of Pegu. The reply they received from Lord Dalhousie was eminently characteristic. " Tell them," he said to the interpreter, " that as long as that sun shines in the heavens, so long shall

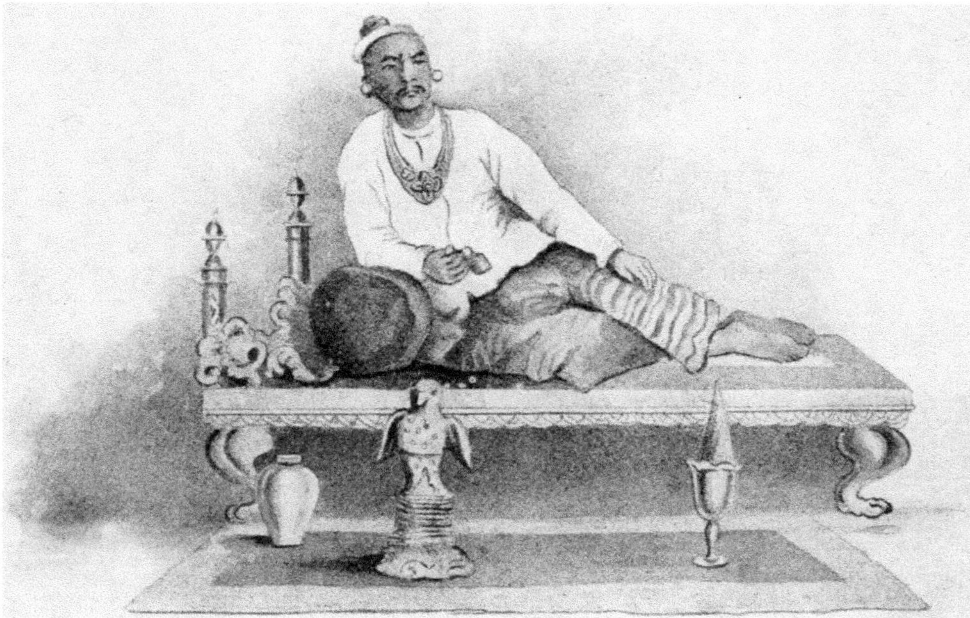

KING MINDÔN MIN

From an old portrait dated 1873

the British flag wave over those possessions." In 1855, a complimentary mission was sent to Amarapura by Lord Dalhousie. Major Phayre was the envoy, and with him were Captain Yule, Dr Forsyth, Mr Oldham, Superintendent of the Geological Survey of India, and some others. This mission was most courteously received, the King expressing the most friendly sentiments towards the British. In 1860, the King moved to the new town of Mandalay, which continued to be the capital until Thibaw's downfall. During the whole of Mindôn's reign, fairly amicable relations were maintained between the Indian and the Burmese governments. The Residents at Mandalay were treated with a fair amount of courtesy; and a court for the trial of civil cases in which British subjects were involved was established in 1869. In the same year, Captain Strover was posted to Bhamo as the first Assistant Political Agent at that place. There were one or two abortive rebellions in Upper Burma, notably one in 1866, got up by some of the King's sons, who resented the appointment of the King's brother instead of one of themselves, as Crown Prince. The King's interferences with trade often caused great discontent on the part of the merchants of Rangoon, Europeans, Chinese, and natives of India, all of whom suffered business losses in consequence at times. But, so long as Mindôn Min lived, matters remained on a very much more satisfactory footing than they had ever been under any of his predecessors.

King Mindôn died on 1st October, 1878, at the age of sixty-four, after a reign of twenty-six years. He had been seriously ill for two months, and during that time there had naturally been much scheming in the palace in regard to the succession. There is no recognised order of succession, and since the death of his brother, who was murdered in the rebellion of 1866, the King had refused to nominate a successor. In 1869, the Resident, Captain Sladen, had urged him to appoint a successor, on the ground that this was the surest way to secure peace. The King replied that it would be the surest way to create disturbances. With so many grown-up sons as he had, to appoint any one of them as Crown Prince, would be practically signing the death-warrant of the prince selected. The question of the succession was therefore left unsettled to the last. It would have been a very difficult question to settle at any time. In India, as Mrs Steel points out in her "India through the Ages," the failure of heirs recurs constantly in a way that is both pathetic and suggestive. In Burma, on the other hand, the trouble was generally due to the superabundance of heirs. When Colonel Horace Browne was in Mandalay as Resident, about a year after Mindôn's death, he, with the assistance of Raj Singh, astrologer and horoscopist to the royal family, compiled a list of the members of the royal family at the time of Mindôn's death. Raj Singh was not quite confident about the number of grandchildren, as he had not been called on to officiate at the birth of all of them ; but, so far as the wives and children were concerned, he guaranteed the correctness of his list. King Mindôn had married fifty-three wives. Twelve had predeceased him, and one, Thibaw's mother, had been divorced for infidelity. She had carried on a *liaison* with a monk, and under any other King but Mindôn would probably have been punished in a more drastic fashion than by divorce only. When Mindôn died, he left forty disconsolate widows and one hundred and ten surviving children. Including the grandchildren, Raj Singh estimated the approximate number of Mindôn's surviving descendents at three hundred.

Of the children, forty-eight were sons, but of these two were in exile, having fled after the failure of their rebellion in 1866. The remaining forty-six sons were all possible successors, though some of them had a somewhat better claim than others, owing to the superior rank of their mothers. But there was no one with an absolutely outstanding claim to carry him through ; and no one who might not aspire to the throne with some hope of success, though those who were still under eighteen years of age, and whose succession would have involved a regency, stood a very poor chance, no doubt. Still a clever mother might have managed the succession even of a minor, though it would have been difficult. As it was, the one who did succeed, being the only one whose mother had been put away for infidelity, seemed to be the most unlikely of all to succeed.

So far as any rights of preference existed at all, the three princes who had the best claim were the Mekkhara, Thônzè, and Nyaung Yan princes. They were all loyal ; they had rendered equally good service in the rebellion of 1866 ; they were much of an age, and, as far as their mothers were concerned, they were on an equality according to Burmese notions. On the 12th of September, less than three weeks before the King's death, the princes received an order to attend the King. The mother of the Nyaung Yan prince warned him not to obey the order, so he and his younger brother took refuge in the British Residency. The other princes obeyed without suspicion, but were arrested and imprisoned. Their mothers managed to convey the news of this to the King ; he ordered their release, and summoned them to his presence. The Mekkhara prince explained to his father what had occurred, and Mindôn realised their danger. His method of averting this danger was to appoint each of the three leading princes regent of a specified third of the country. After the King's death each of them was to rule his own territory independently, and the remainder of the royal family were to be free to attach themselves to any one of the three they preferred. The King issued the necessary orders for this, and the princes retired, but when they reached the north garden, they were again seized and thrown into prison. Their mothers and sisters tried to reach the King to tell him what had happened, but the Alenandaw Queen, who was the originator of the plot, met them, bade them hold their peace in the palace, and they soon found themselves prisoners in their own apartments. Meantime, the King was congratulating himself on having saved his sons, and thought of them as "going full of joy and gratitude to assume their new duties." Apparently he was allowed to cherish this delusion until his death.

The Alenandaw Queen's plan was as follows. She knew the King was dying; and she knew also that each Queen would intrigue for her son, with the aid of any officials she could win over. The Alenandaw Queen was hated by most of the royal family; she had no son of her own to intrigue for, but Thibaw was in love with her daughter Supayalat, and he was only twenty years of age, old enough to do without a regent and young enough to make it probable that, through her daughter, she would still be able to exercise a predominant influence for some years to come. She won over the Kin Wun Mingyi and other less prominent officials, by pointing out that the triple regency devised by the King must result in disturbances, and the overthrow of the ministers themselves. She, therefore, suggested that all the princes should be confined as a precautionary measure. At the same time she hinted that the King had expressed a wish that Thibaw should marry Supayalat, and should be appointed heir. None of them were in the least likely to believe the latter statement, but they were quite alive to the dangers likely to arise on the King's death, so they fell in with her plan. To avert suspicion, and to persuade the people that the arrest of the princes was a measure of precaution for the tranquillity of the country, Thibaw was arrested with the others, but he was soon released on the pretext that the King wanted him to give him his medicine. The next step was to get a vote for Thibaw; so, when the ministers were sitting in council, a list of the princes was handed in, and the ministers were requested to put a mark against the name of the one they considered to be the most suitable successor. The President handed it to the Kin Wun Mingyi, who at once put his mark against Thibaw's name. The others, whether in the plot or not, followed suit. It would have been dangerous to do otherwise. Moreover, they all would fully appreciate the reasoning that a lad of twenty was more likely to be manageable than an older man. The Alenandaw Queen claims to have laid this unanimous vote before the King. That she really did so while he was conscious may be doubted. During a slight temporary revival of his strength, she had great difficulty in keeping the ministers from releasing the imprisoned princes.

The day after Mindôn's funeral, Thibaw was proclaimed King. So far, the plot had been carried out with success, but it miscarried grievously in another aspect. The plotters had reckoned without Supayalat. They had been correct in their estimate of Thibaw's character. He could have been influenced easily enough, and might have been as clay in their hands, but Supayalat soon took that work into her own hands entirely, and became the autocratic ruler of the country. An attempt was made by the ministers to start what was called a constitutional system. They established a council and laid down a rule that no order was to be made and no appointment made without the consent of the council, which endeavoured also to keep a control over the treasury. This council lasted for three months only, being summarily dissolved when one of its members ventured to protest against the royal extravagance. This attempt to cut the privy purse was too much for Thibaw, or rather, for Supayalat, and no more was heard of constitutional government.

Immediately after the coronation ceremony, a number of Mindôn's queens, with their daughters, were confined in the palace enclosure near the western gate, and there they remained, closely guarded, until they were released by the British troops, seven years later. As to the princes, who had been secured before Mindôn's death, a large jail was commenced for their accommodation on the western side of the palace, but before long the Alenandaw Queen, Supayalat, and their confidential advisers, came to the conclusion that a simpler, cheaper, and more effectual method of preventing them from giving trouble, would be to kill them all. Thibaw was soon brought round to this opinion, so this hideous massacre was perpetrated in February, 1879. A huge trench was dug to receive them all, and many were tossed in only stunned by the blows of the executioners. Earth was shovelled in over the dead and dying, and the whole was trampled down by the feet of the executioners. After a day or two the surface began to rise again, so all the palace elephants were sent to trample it level again. After some time the trench was opened and the bodies removed to the common burial ground. In this massacre there were several queens and princesses, as well as most of Thibaw's brothers, the total number of victims being estimated at eighty. Both the country and the court were horrified, but none dared to murmur. A spirit of lawlessness, however, soon arose, and dacoits and robbers infested every part of the country.

The extraordinary influence Supayalat obtained over Thibaw is best exemplified by the history of her domestic relations with him. It is not a pleasant story, but its narration is necessary to a complete understanding of his short but disastrous reign. It had always been the custom for the Kings of Burma to have four principal queens, and as many minor ones as they might fancy. Everyone assumed that King Thibaw would follow this custom, and, in order to have two strings to her bow, the Alenandaw Queen managed to get her daughter Supayagyi, as well as her daughter Supayalat, married to the young King. Thibaw's mother, who had re-appeared, of course, on her son's unexpected succession, and the ministers, joined in arranging this double marriage, and the two new queens sat one on his right and the other on his left hand, at the coronation ceremony. Supayalat had not yet realised her power, and could not prevent this. Supayagyi, as the elder sister, moved into the apartments which had been occupied by Mindôn's chief queen. Supayalat established herself in the King's own rooms, and took care never to let him go anywhere without her. The King, therefore, saw nothing of Supayagyi at all. For a time Supayalat had to content herself with thus isolating her sister, but she was determined to take the first chance of getting rid of her altogether. The chance soon came. Supayagyi fell sick, and her favourite nurse, Ma Pwa, lighted some candles as an offering to the spirits for the Queen's recovery. Supayalat promptly told the King that Supayagyi and her nurse were working spells for his overthrow. He sent messengers to ascertain what was going on in Supayagyi's rooms. They returned and said candles were burning in a row, but they did not know what the object was. Thibaw was gradually worked into a state of alarm, and had several hot altercations with the Alenandaw Queen, who took the part of her elder daughter. In the end Thibaw ordered the nurse, Ma Pwa, to be put to death. The Alenandaw Queen then became alarmed about Supayagyi's safety, so moved this daughter back to her own immediate care, while Supayalat reigned alone in the palace without any rivals. Supayagyi meanwhile worked herself into such a state of misery over the sentence of death on Ma Pwa, that the Alenandaw Queen again bearded Thibaw and got the death sentence remitted. She could not, however, get her released. Supayalat effectually barred that. Poor Ma Pwa, her three sons, and her aged mother, remained in prison for some months; then Ma Pwa was sent to a prison in Sagaing, and there she was starved to death, in obedience to a private order. Rightly or wrongly, Supayalat believed that Ma Pwa had been scheming to introduce the King into Supayagyi's chamber, so she hated her with a deadly hatred.

In all the dealings in regard to her sister, it is evident that Supayalat had not to contend against any inclination on Thibaw's own part. He had married Supayagyi, as he was directed to do, but was, evidently, quite indifferent to her. Supayalat had soon to face a more formidable rival. When her first child, a daughter, was born, all the daughters of the officials were ordered to come and do homage to the infant. Among them was Mi Hkingyi, who was very good-looking and very gentle in her manner. She was one of those chosen to attend on the child. The King thus saw her often, and took a fancy to her. He told the girl's father that he wished to marry her. The father and mother expressed their sense of the honour intended, but said they were afraid of Supayalat, who would take revenge on the girl and on all her relations. By this time, Supayalat was expecting her second confinement, so the marriage to Mi Hkingyi was arranged secretly, the King promising on his royal honour that he would protect the girl and her relatives, and would proclaim the marriage immediately after Supayalat's second child was born. Not only the Kings but the princes also of Burma had been in the habit of taking a new wife as lightly as they would buy a new pony, so all this fuss and concealment about Mi Hkingyi must have struck her relatives as very absurd. When the King did not dare to tell Supayalat at once, his promise of protection could scarcely be implicitly relied on, but it might have proved even more dangerous to refuse than to accept, so the relatives and the poor girl herself had little choice in the matter.

Supayalat was told that the King was going to keep a solemn fast for seven days. She immediately determined to keep one also. Two temporary palaces were erected, in one of which Supayalat kept a genuine fast, while in the other Thibaw spent a sort of honeymoon with Mi Hkingyi. Supayalat was very proud of her own and her husband's asceticism, and boasted loudly that even the pious Mindôn had never submitted himself to such mortification as young Thibaw had just done. A fortnight later Supayalat's second child was born, and Thibaw then told her of the marriage with Mi Hkingyi. Naturally her anger at having a rival was inflamed to fury by the trick about the fast. While she was boasting about Thibaw's asceticism, her attendants must have been secretly laughing at her, as they knew about Mi Hkingyi all along, but had been threatened with death if they told Supayalat. She demanded that Mi Hkingyi should be surrendered to her at once, but this Thibaw summoned courage to refuse. He was still so much afraid of Supayalat, however, that he moved Mi Hkingyi to a safer place in the southern garden of the palace, and she used to visit him dressed in men's clothes and guarded on the way by the Yenaung prince and other confidants of the King. Supayalat then changed her tactics, affected acquiescence in the arrangement, said it would be more seemly for the new Queen to live in the palace, and promised not to molest her. This promise was not kept for long, and when the girl complained to the King, he consulted the Yenaung prince and other confidential friends, as to what he should do. They told him he was entitled to take as many wives as he wished, and recommended thrashing or threatening Supayalat into compliance. Thibaw's mode of acting on this advice showed his inherent weakness of character. On the next occasion of remonstrance with Supayalat about her treatment of Mi Hkingyi, he seized a spear and rushed at Supayalat, who fled to her mother's apartments. Late at night, however, he repented of his hastiness, and went and made it up with Supayalat.

This speedy reconciliation convinced Supayalat that Thibaw was a mere weakling, and that she could do what she liked with him. She returned to the palace with him, of course, but in future quarrels, which were frequent and violent, she never gave way. The result was that between fear of her and love of Mi Hkingyi, Thibaw got into such a distracted state that rumour said he was going mad. Supayalat's next move was to get rid of the Yenaung prince and the other friends of the King,

KING THIBAW AND QUEEN SUPAYALAT

Photograph by Mr Samuels, Mandalay

who had recommended that she should be reduced to subjection by a thrashing or some equally cogent argument. Her method of doing this was to prepare a number of petitions accusing them of treasonable conspiracy, and to arrange matters so that these petitions should appear to come from various sources. The King lived in constant dread of such plots, so was soon persuaded to order the arrest of all his friends, Supayalat taking care that their jailors should be her own creatures. After about three weeks they were all killed or sent into exile. Then began a course of ill-treatment for poor Mi Hkingyi. She was daily nagged at and worried by Supayalat and her maids-of-honour, until her spirit was broken. She was told that if she ventured to go near Thibaw she and her aunt would be accused of attempting magical arts against him, and Supayalat so managed that Thibaw never saw Mi Hkingyi except in public. Under this treatment the King gradually got over his fancy for the girl, so Supayalat was able, first to get her placed under the care of her own chief minion, the Taingda Wungyi, and, later on, to extract from the King what was practically an order for the girl's execution. That order was promptly carried out; Supayalat now reigned alone in the palace, and the control of the country's affairs was virtually in her hands also.

At the time of the massacres, Mr Shaw was British Resident at Mandalay. He protested, and begged the ministers to intervene to save the survivors. In reply he was told that Burma, being an independent country, was entitled to act according to custom; and he was recommended to mind his own business. Early in June, 1879, Mr Shaw died of rheumatic fever, and Colonel Horace Browne, who had served for twenty years in the administration of British Burma, had already been to

Mandalay on various missions, and knew the Burmese well, was chosen to succeed him. Colonel, afterwards General, Browne has published his reminiscences of Burma, and the following extracts from his diary, during the short period of his stay as British Resident, give an excellent idea of the situation. He arrived in Mandalay on 22nd June, 1879.

"June 25th. Some more murders have recently taken place in the palace, the victims being officials, and not members of the royal family. The principal victim was a minister whose offence was casting the Nyaung Yan's horoscope.

"June 27th. I have now been here long enough to survey and take stock of the situation. I find it unsatisfactory from the points of view of our personal safety, the dignity of the Resident, and the utility of his remaining here under present circumstances. My habitation is a tumble-down building with a leaky roof, situated on the edge of a large compound, within which are several smaller sheds occupied by my assistants, the doctor, and the guard. The compound is enclosed and defended (?) by a mat wall, which only requires a few strokes with a hatchet, or a good push with the shoulder to be laid level with the ground. . . . Our great danger is fire. The application of a lighted torch would burn us out in ten minutes. . . . Besides the occupants of the Residency, the whole of the British population now in Mandalay consists of two persons—Mr Colbeck, missionary and chaplain, who, though bereft of his congregation, sticks bravely by his church; and a retired British officer, Major Halsted, who is never seen, and is reported to be of weak intellect. His selection of Mandalay at the present time as a place of residence is almost sufficient proof of the correctness of this report. These two persons form the 'community,' the anxiety for whose safety was the alleged reason which prevented the Viceroy a short time ago from ordering the withdrawal of the Resident, when it was recommended by Aitchison (the Chief Commissioner of British Burma). . . . .

"It is not only from the time of Thibaw's accession that the position of the Resident here commenced to be less satisfactory than it was in former years. The influence and usefulness of the Resident was much impaired from the date, during the old King's reign, when our Government decided to break with the immemorial custom of allowing the Resident to unshoe when going before the King. The fact of the King's envoys to Europe having been admitted to the presence of our Queen with their shoes on, seemed to the then Viceroy a good opportunity for abruptly announcing to the King that the time-honoured custom of the Resident's unshoeing would no longer be complied with. Anyone acquainted with the sentiments of the Burmese court could have informed our Government that the King would certainly take up a *non possumus* attitude on this point, and from that day forward no Resident has been permitted to have an interview with the King. As the old King was his own Minister of Foreign Affairs, and no negociations were ever concluded except at personal interviews with him, this sudden change put an absolute stop to all important business.

"The wisdom of making this revolutionary innovation, without at the same time insisting on the King receiving the Resident with his shoes on, may be doubted. . . . . The frequent visits of former Residents to the palace, and their unconstrained intercourse with the King and his entourage, formed the best, and, indeed, the only means of ascertaining exactly what was going on outside our rampart of mat walls. Now all the information we get is obtained by surreptitious and underhand means. I am even in a more unfavourable position for getting information than was my predecessor up to a few weeks ago, for there has been a general exodus of all respectable Britishers from the capital. Dr Williams was the last to go. From his knowledge of Burmese, from his having formerly been Resident here, and from his subsequent dealings with the King, he was a valuable source of information for Mr Shaw; now he has gone, there is no one to replace him. . . . There is a numerous colony of French and Italian adventurers here, most of them in the service of the King; but even those who are not actively working against English interests shun all intercourse with the Resident. . . .

"As to the actual government here, there appear to be two distinct ones. The first is that of the dissipated boy-King and his termagant wife, who is generally supposed to be more responsible for the policy pursued than the King himself. Her great influence over him is shown by the fact that she has hitherto prevented him from taking the regulation number of wives considered necessary for the royal dignity. These two are surrounded by the palace clique, all more or less implicated in the bloody tragedies which have signalised the present reign. The second party is headed by the Prime Minister, whom Thibaw is afraid to dismiss lest he should declare openly for the Nyaung Yan. . . . No love is lost between these two parties, and each is afraid of the other. The palace party is always breathing fire and slaughter, and would like nothing better than to clear away the Resident, and declare openly against the British. The recent military reinforcements in British Burma have had a slightly sobering effect on these bellicose designs. The

Prime Minister, who has travelled, and is not so ignorant as the others of the relative strength of the two Powers, would not take part in such a policy; but his position is almost as precarious as our own. We are living on the slope of a volcano, unable to peer over the edge into the crater, and with no reliable seismograph to warn us when an eruption is likely to take place."

These extracts from Colonel Browne's diary give some idea of the position in Mandalay a few months after Thibaw's accession. He goes on to report the institution of State lotteries, from which the palace clique realised large sums of money, but at the cost of demoralising the people. Executions went on almost daily, and it was said that Thibaw was in the habit of asking every morning, "Who is there to kill to-day?" Colonel Browne made some efforts to get the sufferings of the imprisoned princesses mitigated, at least, but with little or no success. He remonstrated also about Burmese encroachments in Karennee, to which Lord Dalhousie had promised independence of Upper Burma. The encroachments were made under cover of trading in timber, but, of course, no satisfaction could be got from the court at Mandalay. At last, towards the end of August, Colonel Browne received permission from the Viceroy to leave Mandalay, his assistant, Mr. St Barbe, remaining in charge. A month later, even the Viceroy was convinced that the retention of a Residency at Thibaw's capital was both useless and dangerous, so Mr. St Barbe and all the staff left. On October 12th, Colonel Browne chronicles in his diary Mr. St. Barbe's return to Rangoon, and adds:—

"So at last Thibaw is to be left to 'stew in his own juice,' How long will the process last? It may be a lengthy one, but I give him only up to the end of the reign of the present Viceroy. If it lasts so long, I shall not be here, I am sorry to say, at the final settlement of accounts."

Colonel Browne under-estimated the forbearance of the British Government when, in October, 1879, he gave Thibaw's government only to the end of the existing Viceroyalty as the probable term of its continuance. Thibaw was allowed to continue his course for six years longer, during which time things went steadily from bad to worse. British subjects, travellers and traders from Lower Burma, were subjected to insolence and violence by local officials in Upper Burma. The demoralisation of the people increased until the whole country was harried by dacoits, the Taingda and some other ministers being admittedly in collusion with the dacoits, sharing their gains and frustrating any attempt to suppress these bands. The disorder near the frontier was a standing danger to the peace of British Burma. There were risings in the Shan States; Bhamo was captured and held by a band of Chinese marauders; and a force of fifteen hundred men ravaged the country to the north of Mandalay. At the same time, the Burmese Government was endeavouring to make alliances with foreign powers, more particularly with France. M. Ferry admitted to Lord Lyons that the Burmese had tried to make an alliance, offensive and defensive, with the French Republic. This France refused, but negotiations were entered into for the construction of railways and the establishment of a bank in Upper Burma by French syndicates. Both these agreements are believed to have actually been concluded and signed in Mandalay, and were to be taken to Paris for completion there. If they had been ratified, French influence would have been paramount in Upper Burma, and an intolerable position would have arisen.

There was another hideous massacre in Mandalay in 1884, which raised a storm of indignation in Lower Burma, both Europeans and Burmese protesting against such cruelties being any longer tolerated. To disguise the real character of the massacre a pretended escape from jail was arranged, and the massacre was represented as the suppression of this outbreak. In it between two and three hundred persons, including two princes and many women and children of rank, were brutally butchered. It was early in 1885 that the arrangements for a French railway and a French bank in Upper Burma were negotiated; and at the same time the Burmese Government imposed a fine of twenty-three lakhs of rupees on the Bombay Burma Trading Corporation, a company of timber merchants, chiefly British subjects, working forests in Upper Burma under contracts with the Burmese government. The Chief Commissioner of British Burma asked the King to refer the matter to impartial adjudication, but this was peremptorily refused. At the same time the French Consul in Mandalay offered to take up some of the contracts for the forests, should the Corporation's contracts be forfeited.

It was evident that matters could not be allowed to drift any longer, so an ultimatum was sent to Mandalay, on 22nd October, 1885, demanding three things; firstly, that an envoy should be suitably received at Mandalay, and that the dispute with the Corporation should be settled in communication with him; secondly, that all action against the Corporation should be suspended until the envoy arrived; and, thirdly, that for the future a British Resident should live at Mandalay and should receive becoming treatment from the Burmese Government. On 9th November a reply was received which was practically an unconditional refusal of the terms offered. Three days after the reply was written, and two days before it reached Rangoon, King Thibaw issued a bombastic proclamation to his subjects. The following passage in it is worth recording:—"Those heretics, the English *Kala* barbarians, having most harshly made demands calculated to bring about an injury and destruction of our religion, the violation of our national traditions and customs, and the degradation of our race, are making a show and preparation as if about to wage war with our State. They have been replied to in conformity with the usages of great nations, and in words which are just and regular. If, notwithstanding, these heretic *Kalas* should come and in any way attempt to molest or disturb the State, His Majesty, who is watchful that the interests of our religion and our State shall not suffer, will himself march forth with the Generals, Captains and Lieutenants, with large forces of infantry, artillery, elephanterie, and cavalry, by land and by water, and with the might of his army will efface these heretic *Kalas*, and conquer and annex their country. All royal subjects, the people of the country, are enjoined that they are not to be alarmed or disturbed on account of the hostility of these heretic *Kalas*, and they are not to avoid them by quitting the country."

Thibaw made no attempt to carry out the promise to march out with his forces to efface the British. That was all mere bombast. There was no opposition worth speaking of to the advance of the British force, which crossed the frontier on the 14th November, just a week after the issue of Thibaw's proclamation. There was a slight brush when Minhla was captured on the 17th, during which Lieutenant Drury and three sepoys were killed, and Major MacNeill, three lieutenants and twenty-three sepoys were wounded. Pagan was taken on the 23rd, without opposition ; at Myingyan, which was taken on the 25th, two men of the Naval Brigade were wounded. Some preparations had been made to block the river channel, which, had they been carried out, would have seriously delayed the advance on Mandalay, but they had not been carried out, so the brush at Minhla, and the feeble and futile opposition at Myingyan, practically was all the "war." As compared with the resistance that had been made in 1824-26, and in 1852, that of 1885 was absolutely childish. King Mindôn, as we have seen, did nothing practical to keep up an army. He was eminently peaceful, and his so-called army could never have been of any real account in actual war. Thibaw, or Supayalat rather, was bellicose enough, but they were both far too ignorant to realise the danger they so persistently provoked, or to understand what steps were necessary to secure an effective army.

Before the British force reached Ava, a Burmese envoy came to meet it, and after some negotiation, the unconditional surrender of the capital and of the royal family was arranged. On 3rd December, less than a month after his proclamation, King Thibaw, the Queens Supayalat and Supayagyi, and the Queen-mother, were prisoners on board the steamer *Thooriah*, on their way to Rangoon. The total collapse of Burmese resistance put the Government of India into a difficulty. The King of Burma was a prisoner in Rangoon before it had been decided what was to be done with him. He could not be kept indefinitely a prisoner on board a steamer in the Rangoon harbour, so he was sent with his family, first to Madras, thence to Ranipet, and finally to the old Portuguese fort of Ratnagiri on the western coast of India. There he has remained for over twenty years now, and, presumably, he and his amiable consort, Supayalat, have now grasped some conception of the might of the power they so recklessly defied. Whether they have repented of the barbarous crimes committed during their few years of rule is unknown to the public at large.

CHAPTER XIII.

A.D. 1885 TO 1900

HAD the surrender of the Burmese army been followed up at once by its disarmament, the probability is that the last Burmese war would have been over at once, and that the pacification of the country would have been a comparatively easy matter. The people had no love for Thibaw, and still less for Supayalat. Any sentimental attachment to the Alompra dynasty did not prevent numbers of them from migrating to British Burma when they could smuggle their families across the frontier. They did this even during the reign of a good King, such as Mindôn, and the temptation to do so in Thibaw's time must have been much greater. His appeal to them in his proclamation not to quit the country seems to show that even he realised that many of them would wish to do so, and might take advantage of the war to effect this purpose. In Upper Burma, they were practically the King's slaves, with no tangible rights at all, and subject, not only to royal caprices, which might be avoided by obscurity or by distance from the capital, but also to the caprices of local officials, whom it was impossible to avoid altogether. In British Burma, on the other hand, though there might be petty tyranny on the part of subordinate officials, this had to be done secretly, and the man who was living honestly had little to fear from it. The Government was sincerely anxious to administer even-handed justice to all, and did secure to the poorest such security of life and property as had never been known under the native Kings.

Unfortunately, the Burmese army was not at once disarmed. The result was that a considerable number of the soldiers, and what was of much greater importance, a large number of guns, went to increase the numbers and the effective power of the dacoit bands which had long been harrying the country. Even under Thibaw, the greater part of the country had drifted into a state closely approaching to anarchy, the unfortunate people being ground between the upper and nether millstones of the tyranny of the Burmese officials and the exactions of the dacoits. With the collapse of Thibaw's Government the power of the dacoits was greatly increased. They became more numerous, were better armed, and were able to pose as "patriots." The defence of Thibaw's Government had been so feeble that the war was over much sooner than anyone expected. General Prendergast suddenly found himself nominally in possession of a country covering 75,000 square miles, seething with anarchy, with no highway except the river, and with no regular organised enemy in the field, but numerous bands all over the country, which had each to be dealt with by itself. His whole force numbered 10,500 men only, which had been amply sufficient to conquer the Burmese army, but was totally inadequate to put down at once anarchy over 75,000 square miles. For that, time was manifestly necessary.

Immediately after the occupation of Mandalay, a provisional government was constituted. All the members of the *Hlutdaw*, the great Council of State, professed their willingness to continue to take part in the government. This was scarcely likely to prove a permanent success, but there was, perhaps, some gain in getting this Council to issue a proclamation ordering the Burmese officials to continue in the regular performance of their duties. The first idea was that there should be no breach of continuity, and that all civil officers, whether British or Burmese, were to work under the direction of the *Hlutdaw*. But before a month was out this idea had to be abandoned. The Chief Commissioner, Mr (afterwards Sir Charles) Bernard, arrived in Mandalay on the 15th December, 1885. On his way he had visited Minhla, Pagan, and Myingyan, where civil officers and British garrisons had been placed to restore confidence and pacify the surrounding country. Soon after his arrival in Mandalay, it was decided that these three districts should be administered by the civil officers already stationed there in direct subordination to the Chief Commissioner, without reference to the *Hlutdaw*. The town and district of Mandalay were also removed from its control. The only Minister of importance removed from office was the Taingda *Mingyi*. He was supposed to be responsible for much of the maladministration in Thibaw's reign, had a chief hand in the massacres, and was believed to be very hostile to British interests. He was therefore deported to Cuttack.

On 1st January, 1886, the annexation of Upper Burma was announced, and in February, Lord Dufferin visited Mandalay to consult with those on the spot as to the best method of dealing with the newly acquired province. The *Hlutdaw* ceased to exist as a Council of State, or to exercise any executive or administrative functions. Seeing the character of most of the men who composed it, many of whom were said to have been secretly in league with the dacoits in Thibaw's time, possibly afterwards also, it was scarcely likely that the institution would accommodate itself to British methods. There were some exceptions, however, so a few of the Burmese ministers were retained as advisers to the Chief Commissioner in matters connected with the former government. One or two of those thus retained did loyal service during the remainder of their lives.

Even in Mandalay itself the introduction of order was no easy matter. Under the Burmese Government, a very considerable number of the residents of Mandalay were officials, hangers-on of the Court, and soldiers. Some of the last class went to join the dacoits, but enough remained to form, along with others whose livelihood had depended, directly or indirectly, on the Court, a large class who were thrown out of employment by the change of government. Thus the elements of disorder even in the capital itself, were at once greatly increased. It was only by degrees that the police were able to break up the gangs of robbers, and reduce the town itself to some sort of order. In April they had to deal with the first and only attempt at an organised rebellion, and even that was a feeble affair in which very few were concerned. Some thirty or forty men, professing to be adherents of the Myingun prince (then a refugee in Pondicherry) rushed a police-station, cut down two or three of the policemen, killed a harmless European apothecary who was walking to the hospital, and set fire to some houses in the city, while confederates fired others outside the city walls. These valiant men, however, fled immediately the troops and police turned out. Fires, many accidental, but others, undoubtedly, the work of incendiaries, continued until the advent of the rains. Then the Irrawaddy rose to a greater height than had been known for sixty years, burst through the embankment that had been built by King Mindôn, and flooded the town, rendering many people absolutely destitute. Relief works were at once started, and these did much to secure the good-will of the people. In face of active help of this kind in the time of their distress, it was impossible for them to continue to believe that the British Government was unsympathetic to the Burmese people.

Mandalay town was thus reduced to something like order by the end of 1886, but, beyond the limits of the town, Mandalay district was still almost entirely in the hands of three or four dacoit leaders, who had large followings, and acted to some extent in concert. The territorial limits of each one's jurisdiction were defined and respected by the several leaders. The villagers were made to pay blackmail, and disobedience of orders, or any attempt to help the British Government, were severely punished. An emissary from the Myingun Prince, or, at least, a person who styled himself a Viceroy for that Prince, more or less controlled all these bands, giving them information, and arranging combinations between them. In January, 1887, several Europeans connected with the timber trade, who had then returned to their work, were murdered by these bands within twenty-four miles of Mandalay. The breaking up of these gangs took time to accomplish, but by steady perseverance, and with only occasional assistance from the troops, the district was freed from all these leaders. Three were killed, seven were captured, and twenty-five surrendered. The last of them who gave any serious trouble was pursued in the early months of 1889, and every member of his gang was either killed, captured, or compelled to surrender, though the leader himself escaped. As the dacoit bands were hunted down, trade increased, and the revenue collections also. In 1887-88, the value of the merchandise brought into Mandalay by the Hsipaw route was four and a half lakhs of rupees. The following year it was nearly seven and a half lakhs. By 1889, the town and district of Mandalay were more peaceful and secure than they had been during all Thibaw's reign, and dacoity and cattle-lifting had never been so rare.

What occurred in the Mandalay district is practically the same as what occurred in every other district of Upper Burma. At first, after the collapse of the Burmese Government, dacoit bands held the country, sometimes in the name of a princeling of the Alompra dynasty, sometimes not. King Thibaw's massacres had left no princes of any real importance in the country. The Myingun Prince had been an exile for about twenty years, and the other princes whose names were used by the dacoit bands were very obscure princelings indeed. Many were impostors pure and simple. It was a time when any obscure individual of an adventurous disposition, and with no scruples of conscience, thought he saw a chance of doing something for himself—possibly of gaining a throne. If he could establish a claim, real or bogus, to royal descent, that increased his chances, but many worked quite successfully for a time without this. Ex-officials secured a following, on the plea that they were defending their country; and several monks added to the confusion by working in the name of the national faith. Doubtless there was genuine feeling in some cases, but there was also a good deal of personal ambition, of dislike to seeing law and order firmly established, and of a desire to pluck some personal advantage out of the general chaos. Upper Burma had not only the anarchic elements which had been bred by Thibaw's misrule, but it had also been for many years, ever since the annexation of Pegu in 1852, the refuge for outlaws of all kinds from Lower Burma. The amount of genuine patriotism and of reverence for the national religion, which were mixed up with the prevailing disorder, may be measured by the fact that by far the greater number of these princelings, ex-officials and monks joined the dacoits who had been preying on the country for years before King Thibaw's fall.

The hunting down of all these bands was a wearisome process. Small parties of troops and police were at work all over the country, but it took years before the work was fully done. As Sir George Scott says :—" That was a perpetual record of acts of gallantry which passed unnoticed, because they were so constant ; of endless marches by night and by day, through dense jungle, where paths could hardly be traced, over paths which were so deep in mud that men could hardly march over them and animals stuck fast, over stretches where no water was to be found and nothing grew but thorn-bushes, over hills where there were no paths at all ; and with all this, but rarely the chance of an engagement to cheer the men, stockades found empty, villages deserted, camps evacuated, endless disappointments, and yet everywhere the probability of an ambuscade in every clump of trees, at every turn of the road, from each stream-bed, line of rocks, or ravine. The difficulties were also greatly increased by the fact that by far the greater portion of the country was absolutely unknown, and that for long it was difficult to get competent guides, in some cases owing to the want of good-will on the part of the inhabitants, but far too often because of the treatment the guides afterwards met with at the hands of the dacoits or their friends. Many were murdered, others had their ears cropped off ; the more lucky only had their cattle stolen and their houses burnt."

The losses on the British side were very much greater in this fight with prevailing lawlessness than those in the actual war with King Thibaw. But the fight was steadily pushed on by British troops, by Indian sepoys, by Burmese police, under the guidance often of civil officers It was not until 1890 that order was sufficiently established to admit of any considerable reduction in the strength of the military police. In 1889 the cost of the military police had been nearly sixty-eight lakhs of rupees ; by 1895, it was reduced to a little over thirty-two lakhs.

In addition to Burma proper, the Shan States had also to be brought into subjection. There, however, the task was easier in one way, as the chiefs retained their authority, and, once they had been won over to accept British instead of Burmese suzerainty, it only remained to gradually bring them to rule in a more civilised way than they had been accustomed to. There it was not absolute anarchy we had to face, but we had to deal with a great number of petty principalities, always at war with each other, and never very submissive to the Burmese yoke. Such authority as the Burmese had wielded steadily declined during King Thibaw's rule. The first to revolt had been the Sawbwa of Keng Tung. He objected to an appointment made by King Mindôn, and when King Thibaw confirmed the appointment, the Sawbwa of Keng Tung executed the Burmese Political Officer resident at his court, and massacred the majority of his guard, about thirty in number. He then installed his own candidate, who was subsequently taken under Chinese protection. Then the Sawbwa of Môug Nai, rendered desperate by repeated demands for money, also revolted and massacred the Burmese guard at his capital. One or two smaller chiefs joined him, but the territories of all these were more accessible to the Burmese, so they were driven to take refuge in Keng Tung. There they hatched a plot to set up a prince of the Burmese royal house, in Thibaw's place, or as an independent sovereign of the Shan States. For this purpose, they selected the Limbin Prince, a nephew of King Mindôn, who had escaped to Lower Burma on King Thibaw's accession, been educated at Rangoon, and had been employed by the British Government for some time as a *Myoôk* or subordinate Magistrate. He was removed from this appointment for incompetence, and because he had tried to raise a rebellion in Upper Burma. In October, 1885, he left for Keng Tung, and the allies collected their forces to carry out their project, but meantime King Thibaw had been overthrown by the British, the Burmese troops had been withdrawn from the Shan country, and the whole situation was changed.

British Superintendents were appointed to different parts of the Shan States, and Sir George Scott says :—" Within little over a year after the first occupation of the country, the ruler of every State had made personal submission to the Superintendent, and had agreed to accept his position as a tributary of the British Government on fixed conditions. The intention of the Government to maintain order, and to prevent private wars between the several States, while at the same time allowing to each chief independence in the administration of his territory to the fullest extent compatible with the methods of civilised government, had not only been declared, but had been exemplified. Trade began to revive almost immediately, ruined villages and towns were reoccupied and re-built, and the people began to resume their ordinary pursuits, which it may be said have never since been disturbed, except in the frontier States, and there only for reasons which were purely local and differed in each case."

An account of the pacification of Upper Burma would not be complete without some reference to the part played by the Karens in putting down the anarchy which had overflowed into the British province from the newly acquired territory. Hunted down by the troops in Upper Burma, many of the dacoits crossed the old frontier line and began to attack the villages in Lower Burma. The villagers there, having had over thirty years of peace and prosperity under British rule, were richer, and therefore better worth plundering, than those of Upper Burma. All those who preferred lawlessness to settled order were ready to join the dacoits. Some who did so may have been actuated by a sentimental attachment to the Alompra dynasty, and may have considered themselves patriots. Anyway, patriotism was a good card to play, though in considering the importance to be attached to it, one must remember that these " patriots " had always carefully avoided putting themselves under Burmese rule while it was still in existence. Many of them had, no doubt, actually emigrated in previous years from Upper Burma simply to escape from Burmese rule. Still it is possible that they liked to think that there was a Burmese king in existence, though, for their own part, they preferred to live beyond his jurisdiction. If that is patriotism, we may admit that some of them were prompted by that virtuous motive. But, with the majority, no doubt, the real motive was the love of lawlessness. The irruption of the dacoits from Upper Burma strengthened the forces of anarchy and of sedition, and every young Burman with a taste for adventure saw a chance of indulging that taste, and of acquiring wealth by a more congenial method than that of honest work.

Thus in Lower Burma, as well as in Upper Burma and the Shan States, the British found themselves confronted with the forces of anarchy. A number of dacoit bands had to be hunted down, and the existing police were not strong enough to combat this sudden accession of strength on the part of the lawless classes. Villagers were terrorised, and did not dare to openly help the authorities, lest the neighbouring dacoit leaders should inflict summary vengeance for what they termed treachery. On the other hand, the villagers were forced, not only to feed the dacoits, but to give them information as to the movements of any military or police force sent to hunt them down. The hunt thus became almost hopeless. The troops or police tracked the dacoits to their camp, only to find the camp deserted, and the dacoits scattered in dense jungle. To arm the Burmese villagers was useless. That was only a way of indirectly arming the dacoits, as, on the approach of a dacoit band, the villagers fled, and the dacoits seized the guns.

At this juncture, the Karens, headed by their missionaries, asked to be armed, and volunteered to put down the dacoit bands. The Burmese had always despised the Karens, and, before the time of British rule, had bullied them so terribly that the Karens had taken to living very much in the inmost recesses of the jungle. They therefore were able to follow the dacoits into places where the troops could not go. Of their loyalty there could be no doubt, as they knew well that the overthrow of British rule would mean a return of the old times of misery for them. But the British officials of Lower Burma did not properly appreciate the work which the American Baptist missionaries have done among the Karens. In the course of a generation or two, through Christianity, the Karen tribes have been welded into a nation. They are no longer hunted savages, living in concealment in dense jungle, and hiding themselves at sight of a Burman. They live in comfortable villages,

KAREN GIRLS IN NATIONAL DRESS

BOTH SKIRTS WOVEN BY KARENS. ONE JACKET TRIMMED WITH SEEDS, THE OTHER, VELVET TRIMMED WITH WORSTED

Photograph by Rev. H. I. Marshall, American Baptist Mission, Tharrawaddy

almost every village supporting its own pastor and schoolmaster. They have learned to act in unison in matters affecting their own welfare, even those who have not accepted Christianity joining the Christians in such matters. They have learnt, too, that death is not the worst evil in the world, and they were ready to die, if need be, in defence of their hearths and homes. This they proved afterwards, for when they did eventually get arms, the dacoits were never able to take these so long as the Karen owners lived. But the British officials did not realise this, and were as much taken aback by the demand of the Karens as if a rabbit had suddenly sprung up and demanded arms.

In his book, "The Loyal Karens of Burma," published in 1887, Mr Smeaton, an Indian civilian, who served for very many years in Burma, says :—"The wave of lawlessness and rebellion which swept over Lower Burma immediately after the Mandalay campaign, and which has not yet subsided, was foreseen and foretold by one of the leading Karen missionaries. He warned the authorities that danger was brewing in our own province, and offered to raise a Karen contingent which would keep the rebels in check. The local authorities, however, appear to have ignored the danger, and refused the offer with something akin to a sneer, with what results we now know. Until, in sheer despair, the Karens rose to defend their own hearths and homes, the Burmese rebels and robbers had it all their own way. Troops could not penetrate the dense jungles; and the Burmese police were cowardly where they were not disloyal. The Karens are splendid forest trackers and ruthless pursuers. When they rose vengeance was swift. They tracked the raiders to their hiding places, attacked and routed them, hunted the fugitives from jungle to jungle, and cleared the frontier. There can be no question that, with the peace of the entire province at stake, it would have been the boldest and the best policy to array the loyal Karens, at the very outset, against the rebel bands. A body of five thousand Karen skirmishers, with General Prendergast's invading force, would have cut off the retreat of the Burmese troops, and would have checked the irruption of armed bands into Lower Burma. Much of the anarchy which has disgraced our rule would thus have been prevented. The story of the deeds and sufferings of the Karens in defence of the Queen-Empress's Government in Burma is a deeply interesting one, and deserves an honoured place in the records of the Empire "

Mr Smeaton gives some letters from Dr Vinton, an American missionary, written in 1886, which show how little the officials in Lower Burma really did to utilise the services of the Karens. The following extracts will give an idea of the whole :—

" May 15th. I have been driven to my wits' end to protect my villages. I have been dacoit-hunting literally all the time, and paying my own expenses. Discouragement and officialism have just worn my patience thin. The only comfort I have is that I have succeeded in protecting my villages. You may judge of the encouragement our Karens have received by the fact that three Karens have been arrested for murder, and two actually tried. Their only crime was that they had bravely defended themselves and villages when attacked.

" August 2nd. We are still hampered to death, to get arms to buy. Just on a technical point the other day I was refused permission to distribute a hundred guns I had got out for the Karens. I am now one thousand guns short of making the Karen tracts safe. I showed a high official yesterday, by evidence which even he accepted as correct, that floods of ammunition and arms were pouring across the Maulmain frontier from Siam for the dacoits. Loyal Karens were the only men to be harassed. Dacoits could get cheap and abundant rifles of the most improved American patterns. The Karen alone must pay three times ordinary prices for guns more dangerous to him than to the dacoits. Even this failed to break the spell which the apotheosis of red tape has cast over all Burma.

"August 17th. Had a Karen battalion marched due north from Toungoo, with a British force with them on carts, every Burmese soldier could have been disarmed and killed or captured. As it was, the arms which Gladen failed to take away were used against us. The ammunition and rifles were sent down even to Rangoon for sale. I have seen and handled them myself. . . . . In the first days of the rebellion I was talking with C—, and he laughed at me when I told him I would like nothing better than to raise and command a Karen corps. After spending months with sepoys and these very levies, and seeing the Karens charge, firing one volley, and throwing down their guns and going to close quarters with their huge cleavers, C— came and apologised, saying he was wrong to sneer at men who could fight like that. No one had gauged the unifying power of Christianity, or guessed that these loose grains of sand (the clans) had been welded into a terrible weapon. Men will fight when they know they are *solid*, and no traitors among them.

"August 24th. To illustrate the case of thousands, I mention one whom I helped yesterday. After three months hanging round Government offices, begging for a permit which the Chief Commissioner had peremptorily ordered, he got his permit. More than a month has the poor wretch been hanging round Rangoon to get a 'permission to purchase.' Yesterday I happened to go into the town magistrate's office, and, of course, a few words of vigorous Yankee dialect (I was too mad to talk English) got me the required papers. The poor fellow cried like a child, and knelt before me (you know how much a Karen must feel to do this). He had been a prisoner to the dacoits, and a cross was made for his crucifixion. The dacoits took pains to make the cross Christian, and not Burmese pattern, and he only escaped when the moment had arrived for his crucifixion. He had no idea of escaping with his life, but hoped to win an easier death than crucifixion. He had three shots fired at him within six feet, and plunged through the entire gang, cutting and hacking at him with their swords. This man had served in the field under my own eye in the most gallant manner, and yet this was the treatment he had received from your British idol of red tape!"

These extracts give an idea of the state Lower Burma was thrown into after the collapse of the Burmese monarchy. Dr Vinton speaks bitterly, no doubt, but he had good reason for feeling somewhat bitter at the treatment accorded to the Karens by the Government. It is quite true also that the work done by the American Baptist Mission among the Karens had not been properly appreciated before. In spite of all that the Karens did in 1886, it is doubtful whether that work is properly appreciated even now, nearly a quarter of a century later. Whether one sympathises with missionary work or not, there is no denying the fact that this particular piece of missionary work is amply justified by its results. Of course, it started under particularly favourable auspices. The traditions of the Karens made them ready to accept Christianity, and the missionaries have shown great

A MOUNTAIN KAREN VILLAGE

Photograph by Rev. H. I. Marshall, American Baptist Mission, Tharrawaddy

wisdom and tact in their dealings with these converts. They have fostered the idea of Karen nationality, have taught them that they are as good as the Burmese, and, under British law, have equal rights with anyone else. In a word, in a generation or two they have been changed from hunted savages into civilised men and women, leading orderly, cleanly and God-fearing lives.

The unrest in Lower Burma was gradually put down, and with the pacification of Upper Burma and the Shan States, the trade of the country as a whole began to expand rapidly. By the end of the century there is no doubt that the people throughout the length and breadth of Burma were much better off in every way than they had ever been before. It was possible for every one who was honest and industrious to earn a fairly comfortable living, and his life and property were far more secure than they had ever been before. How far the people realise what they have gained is open to question. Many of them do so, no doubt, more especially those whose industry and intelligence have enabled them to acquire considerable wealth. But among every people probably there is a considerable residue whose want of thrift, of self-control, and of industry, unfit them for industrial success, and among the Burmese this element is by no means lacking. Such persons often think that under different conditions they would have done better. The unsuccessful man is apt to think that under such a government as that of the Burmese Kings, he would have been able to rise to wealth and power. He is probably quite wrong in this supposition. It is more likely that he would have been infinitely worse off than he is now But it is impossible to prove this to him. What is certain is that in the time of the Burmese Kings the unsuccessful in Lower Burma did not migrate in any number to Upper Burma. Then the risks and the penalties of failure in Upper Burma were too clearly in evidence. One might rise to be a powerful minister, but it was much more likely that one would remain in abject poverty. While the choice between Burmese and British rule was open, the migration was all the other way, the only migration to Upper Burma being that of those who had brought themselves within reach of the English criminal law. To them, the Burmese King's territory was a convenient haven of refuge, and they preferred to take the risks of poverty, of oppression, and of sudden death there, to facing the certainty of imprisonment if they remained in British territory.

Now, however, the drawbacks of Burmese rule are apt to be forgotten. A generation has grown up which has never known them, and even those who can remember what Burmese rule really was, are apt to forget the disagreeble parts of it. They remember only that, under it, Burmans could rise to the highest offices of State, and that the road to success was less arduous, involving qualities somewhat different from the plodding industry and steady thrift which are necessary for success under British rule. All life was more of a gamble in fact, and the average Burman dearly loves a gamble of any kind. In addition to the discontent of those who dislike steady industry, and would prefer the short cuts to wealth and power which a less stable rule afforded, there is, probably, also a considerable amount of sentimental regret at the overthrow of the Burmese monarchy. Had it been possible to retain a King in Upper Burma under British control, the Burmese would have been gratified. But this course would certainly have greatly complicated the situation. What between French intrigues in Mandalay and chaos reigning throughout Upper Burma and the

Shan States, the task was hard enough as it was without having a King to complicate matters. Moreover, the house of Alompra was most unpromising material to work on. They seemed never to learn anything by experience, and they would certainly have chafed under tutelage. A chafing and intriguing King might have proved much more difficult to deal with than such discontent as we have to face now, which, after all, is mainly on the part of the least orderly part of the population. With the spread of education and the continuance of established law and order, we may safely count on this disorderly element being steadily reduced, while the growing number of those who have acquired wealth must steadily increase the forces on the side of British rule. The Burmese may have some sentimental regret at the overthrow of the Burmese monarchy, but no man who has any property at stake can seriously wish to have it restored. The British Government gives them security of life and property, and this they never had under a Burmese King, and certainly would not have were the Burmese monarchy restored. With the growing prosperity of the country, wealth is being very widely distributed among the best elements of the people, and, unless our rulers blunder badly, there is no reason to fear for the future. All that is needed is to steadily maintain law and order, to administer even-handed justice to all, and to leave the people alone as much as possible to develop in their own way. Possibly the greatest danger lies in well-meaning enthusiasts of all kinds, who want to play the part of an earthly Providence, and who think that they can abrogate Nature's salutary laws. Their idea is to bolster up the unfit, with consequences which are apt to prove disastrous. Such men are to be found in the House of Commons, where they often do a good deal of mischief, their ill-informed utterances there being read in India and Burma, and taken much more seriously than they deserve. It is difficult for an Asiatic to understand that the opinions of an individual faddist carry no weight, even though he happens to be a member of Parliament. Such men are also to be found in the ranks of the officials, where they can do even greater mischief. A high official has very considerable power, and, if he happens to hold doctrinaire opinions, he can sometimes carry foolish measures designed to protect certain classes from the effects of their own folly. The best check on that would be to give the moneyed classes, both large landholders and the commercial classes, more definite powers of resisting legislation of an objectionable kind. Through the Chambers of Commerce and the Trades Associations the opinion of educated business men can always be obtained, but the officials are not always ready to accept that opinion. Yet the business man can often see, when the official does not, that certain kinds of legislation cut at the very root of all prosperity.

APPENDIX

MOST of the criticisms I have seen on the first edition of this book were merely to the effect that I had straightened out the tangled skein of Burmese history and had put it into readable form for the first time. This was all that I aimed at doing, and it is gratifying to have my success in this direction so generally acknowledged as it has been. In publishing a second edition, however, I wish to make some reply to various criticisms made in Burma, either through the press or by private letters to myself. The book, naturally, attracted more attention in Burma than elsewhere, and I was greatly pleased to find that it had met with the approval of the more intelligent Burmans capable of reading English. One of them told me that until he read this book he had never known the history of his own country. The most important criticism, because it is that of a man who knows the subject thoroughly, and is therefore capable of estimating the correctness or otherwise of Burmese history as I have presented it, was the criticism contributed by Mr Charles Duroiselle, Lecturer in Pâli at the Rangoon College, and published in the *Rangoon Gazette* of 17th March last. It is only right that, in publishing a second edition, any competent criticism on the first one should be brought before the reader.

Mr Duroiselle says :—" But the fact remains that we have had as yet no handbook which the general public might read with pleasure and profit and without fatigue or boredom, and to Mr Stuart is due the credit of having undertaken to supply this want, and he has done his task well." He then goes on to criticise some of the statements regarding the early history of the country in the first two chapters, which cover the period up to the commencement of the eleventh century of the Christian era. Of the remaining chapters he says :—

"The other chapters are a very interesting condensation of matter scattered over many publications, which the majority of readers could not have the leisure, nor perhaps the inclination, to peruse, even if the works were readily procurable. The period of Anawrata and his successors has been most cleverly elucidated from the scholarly but puzzling and fatiguing chapters of Phayre, and forms a whole easy to grasp in its details, leaving a clear impression on the mind. So also is the portion dealing with the relations, early and late, of Europeans with Burma, and the British expeditions and final annexation of the country; books, tracts and pamphlets on these subjects now form a respectable amount of literature, and, overcharged as they are in many cases with extraneous matter, their reading must be very careful and laborious, if one desires to gain a vivid impression of the sequence and inter-connection of events. Mr Stuart has paved the way to an easy understanding of this complex chapter of the history of Burma. The facts of this (in its earlier stages) intensely romantic period are set forth succinctly but clearly, and anyone who has mastered them will be able to tread his way with comparative ease through the maze of the voluminous literature on the subject."

In his criticisms on the first two chapters, Mr Duroiselle objects to the two derivations given on page 4 of the word "Talaing." He is probably quite right in accepting Sir Arthur Phayre's derivation as the correct one. It seems much more probable than the other. It is unlikely that a contemptuous name given by Alompra would have persisted. Moreover, the fact that the Indians in the Malay Peninsula and in Siam are still called Klings, a corruption of Kalinga, of which Talinga, (the Telingâna of Phayre) is a synonym, makes it probable that the Talaings got their name in the same way. Mr Duroiselle is, no doubt, correct also in saying that Dr Forchhammer, and not Mr Gray, is responsible for the derivation of " the down-trodden " said to have been given to the Talaings by Alompra. But Gray repeats this derivation and, apparently, endorses it. While considering Phayre's derivation the more probable one, I do not feel justified in utterly ignoring the other, when it has the authority of scholars such as Dr Forchhammer and Mr Gray.

The point to which Mr Duroiselle takes most exception in his comments on the first two chapters of this book, is that referring to the introduction of Buddhism, pages 13 to 16. He says I am rather vague. I submit that it is impossible to be anything else on a subject regarding which so little is really known. He adds that it can now be accepted as certain that Buddhism originally entered Burma from the north-west, that is, through Manipur and Assam, and in the south from India also, but the period at which this entry was effected has not yet been satisfactorily settled. This is, I think, in accord with all probability, as, Buddhism having arisen in India, it would naturally come to northern Burma through Manipur and Assam, and to southern Burma and Arakan by sea from India. The time of entry I will refer to later. But Mr Duroiselle goes on to say:—"On the other side it is more than improbable, in fact impossible, for Buddhism to have been introduced from the north-east, that is, from the central provinces of China through Yunnan, or from Yunnan itself, for up to the middle of the eighth century A.D., the tribes of Yunnan and Tongking formed a formidable barrier against China, which she was not able to break through for long centuries."

No doubt Yunnan, until it was finally subdued by Kublai Khan in the thirteenth century, was a barrier to much communication between Burma and China. It delayed the crushing defeat which Burma had to endure when she first came in contact with a comparatively strong power such as China was. But a barrier of this kind, though a very real obstacle to commercial relations or to the passage of either a Burmese or Chinese army, would not be a very serious hindrance to individual missionaries, animated by zeal for the propagation of their faith, and willing to face danger and death in that cause. Buddhism was introduced into China in the first century after Christ, and by the fourth century nine-tenths of the inhabitants are said to have been Buddhists. Later on, Buddhist and Hindu ideas were alternately accepted and persecuted in China. The early missionaries who went to China in the first century—probably the pioneers who paved the way for those who made sufficient impression to leave any trace, went very much earlier—as well as all those who must have followed in considerable numbers to bring about so wide an acceptance of Buddhism by the fourth century, must have passed through both Burma and Yunnan. Burma, being so much nearer India than China, would surely be the first field for missionary enterprise, and its conversion, even in part, would facilitate enterprise further afield to Yunnan and then to China. A chain of monasteries throughout the route would render the passage of missionaries backwards and forwards comparatively easy, though Yunnan still remained an insuperable barrier to commercial and warlike expeditions. I am not urging that Burma received its Buddhism from China. It seems so much more probable that Burma received it from India, and that she received it even before China did. I am merely trying to controvert the proposition that an independent Yunnan would be a serious hindrance to the passage of missionaries.

As to Buddhaghosa, whom I have called " the reputed apostle " of Buddhism in Burma, at the same time saying that the story is of very doubtful authenticity as to details, Mr Duroiselle says :—" Really little is known about Buddhaghosa, and his very existence has been doubted. The very monumentality of his work has made some think that ' Buddhaghosa ' was, perhaps, the name of a school, or of a period of renaissance become personified. We would not go so far ; but from the notices of him found in many books, it can certainly be proved he never visited Burma. The remarkable revival of Buddhism which seems to have taken place in the Talaing country in the fifth century is probably to be attributed to nothing else but to the influence of the extraordinary literary activity which was just then renovating Ceylon." Mr Duroiselle also calls Buddhaghosa " the greatest of Buddhist divines " and the " renovator of the Buddhist Church." It is no doubt true that the Talaing claim to Buddhaghosa as a fellow countryman is " against all evidence," as Mr Duroiselle says. There is no evidence that he ever visited Burma or the Talaing country at all. According to the evidence available, he was a native of India, and when his work in Ceylon was finished, it is distinctly stated that he went back to India. Nothing I have said, however, conflicts with this ; and a remarkable revival of Buddhism in the

Talaing country in the fifth century surely suggests the probability of its having been introduced long, possibly centuries, before. The accounts of the early Buddhist missions to foreign countries may be as untrustworthy as Mr Duroiselle says they are, but if these missionaries had made some perceptible impression on distant China by the first century, the chances are that they had done so in the Talaing country, probably in Upper Burma also, even earlier. In missionary enterprise there is much pioneer work to be done before any results likely to be generally recognised are apparent. Even under present conditions this is the case, and two thousand years ago, when the conditions were infinitely less favourable for travel and the spread of ideas than those now prevailing, this pioneer work would be more difficult and would take longer time than it does now. Two thousand years hence but little record may survive of many of the Christian missions of the present day. Such accounts as have come down to us of the Buddhist missions of some two thousand years ago may be very untrustworthy, but the results show that there must have been active propagandist work carried on at the commencement of the Christian era, probably even some centuries earlier.

Mr Duroiselle next takes exception to what I say in pages 14 and 15 about the falling away into heresy in the sixth century. He says that the Aris were the priests, not of Naga worship, but "of that religious medley which was made up of Mahayanism, Tantraism, Shivaism and Naga worship, which existed not only in Burma, but in almost all Indo-China." No doubt this is perfectly correct, but "priests of the Naga worship" expressed the central point of the falling away from Buddhism; and to nine readers out of ten probably the addition of the words Mahayanism, Tantraism and Shivaism would convey no idea whatever. He also objects to the statement that this Naga worship was introduced into Burma in the sixth century. I do not speak of it as having been introduced, but as a falling away from Buddhism, which, of course, is compatible with its being a falling back on an older creed. Mr Duroiselle then goes on to say :—"But it may be urged this very statement of the introduction of Naga worship into Burma in the sixth century is made in the Burmese histories. This is true, but it must be remembered the Burmese Chronicles were composed at the very least eight or ten centuries, and rather more, after this alleged introduction, and therefore the categorical statement (given in the chronicles) that the Aris and their religion came to Burma exactly in 513 A.D. cannot be accepted without further consideration, unless it be admitted the Burmese had a wonderful gift of remembering exact dates. They had not this gift, not even to remembering events which proved nearly a national calamity several centuries later than the seventh. For instance, two invasions from Yunnan recorded in Chinese histories, but so completely forgotten by the Burmese that they are not even mentioned either in inscriptions or in the chronicles. They apparently possessed no help to memory ; for although writing may have been known long before, there is absolutely no proof that the Burmese knew the art of writing before the tenth century."

On several occasions I point out the untrustworthiness of the Burmese chronicles, so I would be the last person to insist on their absolute accuracy on any point. But some general idea of the truth may be gained, even from an untrustworthy witness, when one knows his bias. We know that facts are twisted or suppressed altogether when they wound the national vanity of the

Burmese. The account of the first Anglo-Burmese war as given in the Burmese chronicle and reproduced on page 131, is an example of twisting facts out of all semblance to the truth. The omission of the two invasions from Yunnan, referred to by Mr Duroiselle, is an instance of the suppression of humiliating episodes. It was convenient to forget them, so they were omitted from the chronicle altogether. In the same way, we need not accept as literal truth the account of the introduction of Naga worship, still less its exact date.

But as in later times when Buddhism was the prevailing religion, an introduction of, or a relapse to, Naga worship would not be considered a creditable episode, no Burmese chronicler would be at all likely to introduce it unless he had very tangible ground on which to base the assertion, either in older records or in tradition. There may be no proof that the Burmese knew the art of writing before the tenth century, but it is difficult to believe that it was totally unknown in any country which had embraced Buddhism even partially. The Buddhist missionaries must have introduced it wherever it was previously unknown, and it seems very improbable that the Burmese should have remained wholly ignorant of it right up to the tenth century. Whatever the source may be from which these early chroniclers got their facts, it must have pointed to an increase of Naga worship somewhere about the sixth century, and it was more flattering to national vanity to represent this as an introduction from outside than as the increased devotion to a cult which had never been quite extinct.

Mr Duroiselle then protests against the inference I draw that this mention of heresy in the sixth century points to something like orthodox Buddhism having been known in Upper Burma for some centuries before. Possibly I should not have used the expression "orthodox Buddhism." By this expression he understands Hinayanism or Southern Buddhism, to which, he says, even Northern Buddhists admit the claim to far greater antiquity and orthodoxy. But I was not thinking of orthodoxy in the theological sense. The Buddhism of Upper Burma in these early centuries was probably very far from being theologically orthodox; but even the corrupt form of Northern Buddhism, which Mr Duroiselle admits to have existed then, would be greatly superior to the Naga worship or "medley" religion, as he calls it, which was mixed up with it, or flourished alongside of it. It is quite possible that pure, or orthodox Buddhism was more or less unknown in Upper Burma until Anawrata introduced it from Thaton. Even then, no doubt, the corrupt Buddhism, as well as much religion that was not Buddhist at all, was mixed up with it or existed alongside of it.

It is possibly not literally correct to say that Anawrata had no difficulty in stamping out the heresy, that is, of the Aris. On this point, Mr Duroiselle says:—"Very far from it; he simply introduced from Thaton a very pure form of Buddhism, which went on existing side by side with the other. The histories plainly affirm (and the statement is very strong, as it is done unwillingly, and against the claims of Buddhism itself) that the last effort to stamp out the animal sacrifices, the Aris and Naga worship, was made by Sin Phyu Shin in 1555 A.D., and an inscription dated 1468 is a standing witness of the existence of the Aris and consequently of the medley religion in that year at least. The Naga-Yon Temple at Pagan is another proof that Anawrata in 1057 did not stamp out the heresy. In fact the European, and the Burman of to-day who opens his eyes, can easily see that the Naga has not yet been stamped out of the national art at least, for the Naga is to be seen everywhere in Burma, artistically, but not very much, transformed, in every carving of the pagodas, at the extremity of the common carts, and in pictures and frames. The observant reader will easily detect the cobra (naga) everywhere on the platform of the Shwe Dagon." There is no doubt that, not only in the national art, but in the customs of the people, many relics of an older religion than Buddhism still survive. But this is not peculiar to Burma. As the author of "The Golden Bough" has shown, customs still prevail very widely among the peasants of many nations in Europe which have their origin in the old pagan religions which prevailed before the introduction of Christianity. It is not surprising that the same conditions should still exist, and even in a more marked degree, in Burma, where numerous tribes are still unconverted to Buddhism, and keep alive the recollection of the older and more primitive cults.

Mr Duroiselle's next criticism is :—" I would here protest against the generally accepted theory that King Anawrata, in 1057 A.D., destroyed Thaton from a religious impulse. Anawrata was probably no better Buddhist than his subjects. Everything seems to show that his arms were first directed against the alarmingly prosperous Hindu colonies of the sea-coast, and thence against the ever-growing power of the Talaings, whom he considered a standing danger. His motives were political, not religious." This may be so, but in those times politics and religion were very much mixed up, and it is difficult to determine how far any monarch in the eleventh century was really actuated by the religious motive assigned to such a campaign as that waged by Anawrata, and how far it was merely made the pretext for ambitious designs.

Mr Duroiselle says also that he " does not altogether agree with the proposition that it is owing to Buddhist propagandism that Burma escaped from the fetters of the caste system. The castes have never been firmly established outside India itself, where the Brahmins possessed enormous influence and had the regal power to support them. In Burma their number must always have been comparatively small compared with the rest of the population, and it is rather their amalgamation into the mass of the people that prevented the caste system from taking root." No doubt, the Brahmins could never have had their pretensions acknowledged immediately by an alien people, but they are singularly astute, and had Indian influence been brought to bear on Burma before the Buddhist revolt had weakened their power, they might in time have established their ascendancy in Burma also. Once Buddhism in any form had taken root, the establishment of any such ascendancy became almost impossible among a people who had never known it.

Mr Duroiselle's comment on the second chapter is as follows :—

" The second chapter, which treats of the period extending from A.D. 639 to 1010, is singularly interesting. The author's chief authority for the first chapter is, we think, Mr Taw Sein Ko ; for the second he follows chiefly Mr Parker's " Burma, its Relations with China." Mr Stuart, following Parker, describes the quasi-subjection of the Burmese Kingdom of that time to the Nan-Tchao, a then powerful kingdom occupying the greater part of Yunnan, and whose inhabitants were probably Thais

(Shans) and the influence of the Nan-Tchao on Burma. But he has here followed too closely Mr Parker, for, like him, he does not say a word of the influence exercised by Burma on the Nan-Tchao, an influence easily discernible in the Indianised names of Yunnan and of some of its towns, Gandhara, Mithila, etc.; also in the peculiar way some of the Nan-Tchao kings formed their titles, which is unknown to China and the Thais, but has many parallels in Burma, and in certain Burmese legends which were current in the Nan-Tchao. A study of such influences, intellectual and religious rather than political, would be most interesting. Mr Parker's work is an admirable little book, but we would advise readers to use it with care, especially as regards the geography, for he has not at all rightly apprehended it; and his efforts at derivation are not seldom erroneous." No doubt the influence of two neighbouring countries, such as ancient Burma and Nan-Tchao, would be reciprocal; but I question whether, in the existing state of knowledge on this subject, it is possible to estimate with any accuracy how far each of these two countries influenced the other. It is to be hoped that the Burma Research Society, which has just been started in Rangoon, will in time do much to clear up this and many other obscure points in the ancient history of the country. As to the Indianised names of towns in Yunnan, the early Buddhist missionaries from India may be responsible for them rather than ancient Burma. The Mahomedan Panthays would scarcely bring them, as they only came from Shen-si and Kan-su, and that only some two centuries ago.

The next criticism to be dealt with is one sent to me privately, from Okkan in the Hanthawaddy district, by Mr Palmer. This gentleman points out that I have omitted to mention Marco Polo's references to Burma. The justice of this criticism I fully admit. Some reference to the account given by this early European traveller should have been brought in at the end of the third chapter, as Marco Polo's account is not only quaint and interesting in itself, but refers to an important period, namely that of the total defeat of Burma by the army of Kublai Khan, the fall of Pagan and the complete collapse of the Anawrata dynasty. To repair this omission I now insert the following notes regarding Ser Marco Polo's book concerning "the kingdoms and marvels of the East," taken from Sir Henry Yule's edition of his work.

Marco Polo, the Venetian traveller of the 13th century, has several references to Burma, to which he gives its Chinese name "Mien." It is not certain that he was actually in Burma himself, though he may have been, but he must have been very near it and it is evident that his accounts were obtained from fairly accurate contemporary authorities. If he did not get his knowledge from the Burmese themselves, he at least got it from their near neighbours. He describes a province which he calls Zardandan, the capital city of which, called Vochan, is five days' march from Tali-fu. The men of Zardandan cover their teeth with a sort of golden case, and are illiterate savages, not converted to Buddhism, but practising devil-dancing and other strange rites of Shamanism. It has not been definitely determined who the people here referred to were, but there is good reason to believe that they were the Kakhyens, a wild race still to be found in considerable numbers on the northern frontiers of Burma, though they have given up, if they ever really practised it, the absurd custom of gold cases for their teeth. There is little doubt that Vochan is the city known to the Chinese as Yung-ch'ang-fu, which could be reached from Tali-fu in five days. Zardandan in Persian means " Gold-Teeth." The Chinese geographical work *Fung-yu-ki-yao* mentions Kiu-Chi " Gold-Teeth " as the ancient name of Yung-ch'ang. Baber mentions that he met with the practice of chewing betel with lime first near Tali-fu and suggests that this may be the origin of the name " Gold-Teeth." Betel-chewing is common all over China, but the use of lime is almost unknown, so the teeth are not necessarily discoloured, whereas when lime is added to the chew, the teeth become red. This seems to be more probable than that savages in the thirteenth century encased their teeth in gold plates. Marco Polo winds up his account of the Gold-Teeth with the remark :—" Now that I have told you of the customs and naughty ways of that people, we will have done talking of them and their province, and I will tell you about others, all in regular order and succession."

After describing " the naughty ways " of the Gold-Teeth, Marco Polo goes on to describe what was manifestly the first encounter between the troops of Kublai Khan and the Burmese. His date 1272 is, no doubt, a mistake, but in describing the Burmese king as the King of Mien and of Banagla he may be correct to a certain extent. King Anawrata had extended his conquests to the frontiers of India, and is said to have set up images in that country, though there is no reason to suppose that he ever ruled any part of India. Still it is quite possible that Anawrata and his successors may have arrogated to themselves the title of " King of Bengal." The Burmese kings have always been specially addicted to high sounding titles, and there was nothing to hinder them from calling themselves kings of Bengal if they pleased. It would not have been worth while for the actual rulers of Bengal to dispute it, so long as it remained a mere empty title having no basis in actual existing fact. But there is reason to believe that there was some confusion in Polo's mind between Bengal and Pegu, so he may have meant only Pegu, which was at that time subject to Burma and continued to be so up to the time of the Mongol invasion. The following is Polo's account, given as far as possible in his own words.

"You see, in the year of Christ 1272, the Great Kaan sent a large force into the kingdoms of Carajan and Vochan to protect them from the ravages of ill-disposed people. . . . . Now there was a certain king, called the King of Mien and of Bangala, who was a very puissant prince, with much territory and treasure and people; and he was not as yet subject to the Great Kaan, though it was not long after that the latter conquered him and took from him both the kingdoms that I have named. And it came to pass that when this king of Mien and Bangala heard that the host of the Great Kaan was at Vochan, he said to himself that it behoved him to go against them with so great a force as should insure his cutting off the whole of them, insomuch that the Great Kaan would be very sorry ever to send an army again thither. So this king prepared a great force and munitions of war; and he had, let me tell you, 2000 great elephants, on each of which was set a tower of timber, well framed and strong, and carrying from twelve to sixteen well-armed fighting men. And besides these, he had of horsemen and of footmen good 60,000 men. In short, he equipped a fine force, as well befitted such a puissant prince. It was indeed a host capable of doing great things."

We are then told that to meet this host, the Captain of the Tartar army, named "Nescradin" (probably Nasr-uddin, who is frequently mentioned by Chinese writers as having been employed on this frontier at that time) had only twelve thousand horsemen. "Natheless he was a most valiant and able soldier, of great experience in arms and an excellent Captain." He chose the plain of Vochan, hard by which was "a great wood, thick with trees" and there he awaited the Burmese attack. When the Burmese arrived within a mile of the enemy the king "caused all the castles that were on the elephants to be ordered for battle and the fighting men to take up their posts on them, and he arrayed his horse and his foot with all skill, like a wise king as he was." The Tartars advanced to meet the enemy, but their horses could not be induced to face the elephants, so they dismounted, tied their horses to the trees, and went forward on foot with their bows, "a weapon that they know how to handle better than any troops in the world." They handled them to very good purpose on this occasion. "Understand that when the elephants felt the smart of those arrows that pelted them like rain, they turned tail and fled, and nothing on earth would have induced them to turn and face the Tartars. So off they sped with such a noise and uproar that you would have trowed the world was coming to an end! And then too they plunged into the wood and rushed this way and that, dashing their castles against the trees, bursting their harness and smashing and destroying everything that was on them." Then the Tartars remounted their horses and charged the enemy. The Burmese seem to have stood their ground for some time and to have fought bravely. "The din and uproar were so great from this side and from that, that God might have thundered and no man would have heard it! Great was the medley and dire and parlous was the fight that was fought on both sides; but the Tartars had the best of it. In an ill hour indeed for the king and his people was that battle begun, so many of them were slain therein. And when they had continued fighting till mid-day, the king's troops could stand against the Tartars no longer; but felt that they were defeated, and turned and fled. And when the Tartars saw them routed, they gave chase, and hacked and slew so mercilessly that it was a piteous sight to see. But after pursuing a while they gave up, and returned to the wood to catch the elephants that had run away, and to manage this they had to cut down great trees to bar their passage. Even then they would not have been able to take them without the help of the king's own men who had been taken, and who knew better how to deal with the beasts than the Tartars did. The elephant is an animal that has more wit than any other; but in this way at last they were caught, more than 200 of them. And it was from this time forth that the Great Kaan began to keep numbers of elephants. So thus it was that the king aforesaid was defeated by the sagacity and superior skill of the Tartars, as you have heard."

Chinese annalists give 1277 as the date of this battle, and it is probable that the MCCLXXII. of the Texts was a clerical error for MCCLXXVII. The slipping out of V. is more likely than that Marco Polo was mistaken as to the date of the battle he describes so vividly. The Chinese annalists describe the people of Mien as irritated at calls upon them to submit to the Mongols, and as crossing the frontier of Yung-ch'aug to establish fortified posts. They under-estimated the power of the Mongols, as, some six centuries later, they under-estimated the power of British India.

The Burmese Royal Annals do not mention the defeat at Vochan or any other conflict with the Mongols previous to 1281. In that year they say that ten nobles and a thousand horse came to demand gold and silver vessels as symbols of homage. The envoys behaved disrespectfully, which may have been merely a refusal to take off their boots, a point on which the Burmese kings were always very touchy. Anyway the king put them all to death—a somewhat drastic lesson in politeness. The Burmese admit being totally defeated on this occasion, and being pursued to the place now called *Tarokmau* or " Chinese Point " thirty miles below Prome, but they salve their pride by putting the Mongol army at six million horse and twenty million foot soldiers !

The Pegu Chronicle also mentions that "the Emperor of China, having subjugated Pagan, his troops with the Burmese entered Pegu and invested several cities." But the Chinese annals give no idea of so complete a conquest of the country. They only mention *Taikung*, which is probably Tagaung, or Old Pagan, the most ancient capital of Burma, but Marco Polo's " Mien " must have been New Pagan, the capital at that time.

Marco Polo gives a description of the capital city of Mien, which, he says, " is also called Amien, and is a very great and noble city. The people are idolators, and have a peculiar language, and are subject to the great Kaan."

He then goes on to describe two towers, one of gold and the other of silver, the upper part all girt about with bells, which tinkle in the wind. These are evidently pagodas, and he says of them that " really they do form one of the finest sights in the world ; so exquisitely finished are they, so splendid and costly. And when they are lighted up by the sun they shine most brilliantly and are visible from a vast distance."

He then describes the conquest of Burma, which must have followed the Battle of Vochan. He does not give the date, but both Burmese and Chinese annals put it in the year 1284, so there can be little doubt about this date. Marco Polo's account of the conquest is as follows :—" Now you must know that the Great Kaan conquered the country in this fashion. You see at the Court of the Great Kaan there was a great number of gleemen and jugglers ; and he said to them one day that he wanted them to go and conquer the aforesaid province of Mien, and that he would give them a good captain to lead them and other aid. And they replied that they would be delighted. So the Emperor caused them to be fitted out with all that an army requires, and gave them a Captain and a body of men at arms to help them ; and so they set out, and marched until they came to the country and province of Mien. And they did conquer the whole of it ! And when they found in the city the two towers of gold and silver of which I have been telling you, they were greatly astonished, and sent word thereof to the Great Kaan, asking what he would have them do with the two towers, seeing what a great quantity of wealth there was upon them. And the Great Kaan, being well aware that the king had caused these towers to be made for the good of his soul, and to preserve his memory after his death, said that he would not have them injured, but would have them left precisely as they were. And that was no wonder either, for you must know that no Tartar in the world will ever, if he can help it, lay hand on anything appertaining to the dead."

One of Sir Henry Yule's notes in connection with Marco Polo's references to Burma is as follows :—" I see no sufficient evidence as to whether Marco himself visited the city of Mien. I think it is quite clear that his account of the *conquest* is from the merest hearsay, not to say gossip. Of the absurd story of the jugglers we find no suggestion in the Chinese extracts. We learn from them that Nasruddin had represented the conquest of Mien as a very easy task, and Kublai may have in jest asked his gleemen if they would undertake it. The haziness of Polo's account of the conquest contrasts strongly with his graphic description of the rout of the elephants at Vochan. Of the latter he heard the particulars on the spot (I conceive) shortly after the event; while the conquest took place some years later than his mission to that frontier. His description of the gold and silver pagodas with their canopies of tinkling bells (the Burmese *Hti*) certainly looks like a sketch from the life; and it is quite possible that some negotiations between 1277 and 1281 may have given him the opportunity of visiting Burma, though he may not have reached the capital. Indeed he would in that case surely have given us a distincter account of so important a city."

I have also two letters from Maung May Oung, Barrister-at-Law, in Rangoon, regarding the names given to the Kings of the Alompra dynasty. In the first, dated 14th February, 1910, he writes :—" I have been reading your recent work on Burma—and, pending a closer study of it, I wish to draw your attention to a matter, seemingly trivial, but sufficiently serious to call for correction. On page 97, you say that the fifth son of Alompra ousted him and seized the throne, *taking the name of Bodopra.* Again on page 115, you say :— He was thirty-seven years of age at the time and *took the name of Bagyidaw.* Now Bodopra is only a corruption of *Bo-daw-paya ;* Bo means great-grandfather, and the daw and paya are honorific affixes. Again, Bagyi means an uncle (strictly an uncle who is one's father's elder brother). Is it not significant that the two kings referred to were respectively great-grandfather and uncle of Mindôn Min? Is it not probable that the Burmese chronicles were written during Mindôn's time and that the two sovereigns under discussion were respectfully referred to by their relationship to the reigning king? The Burmese even nowadays object to the names of old people being spoken out. Are there any contemporary references to those kings by name? Sangermano calls the first one Badonsachen. Is 'sachen' the worthy father's rendering of '*thakin?*' I have doubts also about the meaning you give to *Alaung paya,* and am making enquiries. The future Buddha is always called Payalaung, or Paya-alaung-daw, but never Alaung-paya. I have heard that the name was adopted after the king's death, and while his corpse was being taken to his capital. Alaung means corpse." To this, my reply was to the effect that he was probably correct about the "sachen." Sangermano may have used "paya" as the Burmese equivalent of "God," and, if so, he might have objected to apply it to any mortal and so have fallen back on "thakin" as the honorific affix to be appended to the king's name. The curious form it took may have been due to Sangermano being an Italian. I added, however, that I thought that Sangermano's name rather confirmed the idea that Bodopra was a contemporary name. Then it could have had no connection with a great-grandson who was not born till near the close of Bodopra's reign.

To this, I received the following reply:-"Your letter of date. . . . The first two syllables of Sangermano's name for Bodopra represent correctly the Burmese *Badôn*—the name of a town or village of those days.

I am told *thakin* was formerly used with reference to women only—princesses of the blood. But I do not think it improbable that a foreigner would make such a mistake. Besides, I have consulted several well-read friends, and we cannot think of any other interpretation of 'sachen.' As regards my suggestions as to the system of nomenclature, U Hpay (Additional District Judge at Thaton) a well-known scholar, agrees with me, and points to another instance, that of Naungdawgyi—literally 'great royal elder brother.' (Naung meaning elder brother is used even colloquially at the present day, in Tavoy and Mergui especially). That sovereign was the elder brother of his successor. Burmans generally believe that Alompra's name of 'Aungzeya' was actually given him at birth. Similar names, it seems, were in common use. U Hpay also holds that some of his followers actually looked up to Alompra as an embryo-something, not necessarily of Buddha. If the latter, 'paya' would not be used after 'alaung' *cf.* Min-laung, Thagya-laung (laung being the same as alaung). Paya would then be an ordinary honorific affix."

If Aungzeya was a common name among the Burmese at that time, it is, of course, quite possible that Alompra really received this name at his birth. But one naturally regards with suspicion the statement that it was so. Auspicious names given at birth are seldom so amply justified by the subsequent career. As to the nomenclature of the Burmese Kings, Maung May Oung may be correct. I understand from Mr Taw Sein Ko that the Royal Chronicles dealing with the Alompra dynasty assumed their present form during the reign of Mindôn Min. If so, it is quite possible that Bodopra and Bagyidaw were both referred to by their relationship to the reigning monarch. To have named all the monarchs of the dynasty in the same way would have produced hopeless confusion, but if two only were to be treated in this way, the selection of Bagyidaw is peculiar, as his reign was far from brilliant. The selection of Bodopra is more intelligible, but it is unfortunate that the name he was certainly known by during his lifetime should bear so close a resemblance to that which, if Maung May Oung is right, only describes his relationship to his great-grandson. The case of Naung dawgyi the eldest son of Alompra, is also peculiar. On this theory, he is named by his relationship to his immediate successor ; that successor is not named in this way, nor are the two lads who succeeded him. Then we come to Bodopra and Bagyidaw, whose names are capable of being interpreted as specifying their relationship to Mindôn. After them we have Tharrawaddy and Pagan, the two immediate predecessors of Mindôn, who retain as kings the names they had borne as princes. The point raised by Maung May Oung is curious and interesting, but, whatever may have been the origin of these three names, they are likely to be permanent now.

The only other criticism to which I need refer is one sent to me by M. d'Avéra, who objects to the extract from Colonel Horace Browne's diary given on page 168. He expresses regret that I should have repeated a sentence which seems to class all the Frenchmen and Italians then in Mandalay as "adventurers." He points out that many of the Frenchmen in Mandalay could not correctly be called adventurers, but he adds that he himself, General de Facieu, M. Vossion and M. de Trevelac had left Upper Burma as a protest against the massacres which took place in February, 1879. As the passage quoted from Colonel Browne's diary was written four months later, it could only apply to the Frenchmen and Italians still remaining in Mandalay. A few days later M. d'Avéra discovered my reference to General de Facieu, on page 153, which convinced him that I, at least, had no intention of classing all the Frenchmen and Italians who had lived in Mandalay as adventurers. Mr Charles de Facieu also wrote to thank me for the reference made to his father, at the same time expressing his regret that recent writers on Upper Burma have been too prone to class all the Europeans residing in Mandalay during the reigns of Mindôn and Thibaw as disreputable adventurers. He then adds the following account of his father's career:—"My father and his father came out to India in 1840. My grandfather had served in the French Army as Colonel of a regiment of Cuirassiers. My father was, of course, but a young man. Both took service in the Punjab before the annexation. Later on my father served as a volunteer during the Mutiny, and he saw the famous Cawnpore well emptied of its gruesome contents. Father, during the first years after his arrival at Mandalay, did all he could to form an army, but he was thwarted at every step and his efforts met with no success. He then realised that the Burmese Government had not engaged his services to help to form an army, but merely to throw a certain amount of *eclat* on the Court, as it flattered the vanity of the king to see a number of Europeans in his service. You have the honour to be the first Englishman to recognise that all the Europeans at Mandalay were not a disreputable lot as is generally believed." No doubt, they have been loosely referred to in this way, but I question whether any of the writers in question seriously meant to class them all as disreputable adventurers.

Index

A

B

B

C

D

E

F

G

H

I

J

K

L

M

M

N

O

P

P

R

S

T

T

V

W

Y

Z